ROI from CRM

It's about sales process, not just technology

Brian K. Gardner

Gale Media, Inc., Lafayette, CO

Gale Media, Inc.
2569 Park Lane, Suite 200
Lafayette, CO 80026
303-443-5060
www.mdm.com

Gale Media is a market-leading information services and publishing company. Its two business units – Modern Distribution Management and MDM Analytics – provide knowledge products and services to professionals in industrial product and wholesale distribution markets. Since 1967, MDM has been the definitive resource for distribution management best practices, competitive intelligence and market trends through its twice-monthly newsletter, market intelligence reports, books and conferences. MDM Analytics provides proprietary market research and analytic services to profile market share and account potential for industrial products.

Additional editorial support provided by Lindsay Konzak.
Cover design by Jackie McCaffrey Bradley.

ISBN 978-0-9906738-4-2

Contents

Introduction

Industrial sales is in my blood.

My father owned Breard-Gardner Inc., an industrial sales rep firm/distributor. I grew up playing with demo equipment in the back seat of the car while on vacations. I spent hours making the colored indicators on magnetic level gauges change and playing with the pressure gauges and digital thermometers. Eventually, during summers and school breaks, I worked in the warehouse stocking shelves and shipping equipment.

My first experience in inside sales was sitting next to Donna. Donna had customer service and process control knowledge in her bones. Her father and brother were both in the instrumentation field; she probably played with demo equipment growing up, as well. Customers loved her. If she was unavailable, they were always happy to wait. This was not always good for my self-esteem, but it made me stop and pay attention. What made customers want to talk with her?

It was obvious Donna knew what she was doing. She always kept things from slipping through the cracks, even though her desk looked like a hurricane had just hit.

Someone would call in and ask about a specific piece of instrumentation or part or model number. Rather than simply answer the question and hang up, Donna took the opportunity to learn more about why they wanted that product versus another. She would ask what the product was for and about its application. And what other things could the client possibly need related to that product or application?

She was sales through and through. She taught me what value-added selling was. It's more than just a customer's need for a product; it's understanding how they use it and offering solutions. In other words, being an asset to the customer and making their job easier. Once you establish yourself with clients in this manner, you'll have them for life.

She was a master. Donna taught me that customers were the reason we had a job. If you took care of them, they would take care of you.

Breard-Gardner was the U.S. master distributor for a Swiss pressure gauge manufacturer, and I had helped set up the warehouse, did some inside sales and built a pressure gauge filling station for them. That hard work paid off, and they invited me to participate in a summer program to learn more about the manufacturing of pressure gauges in Switzerland in 1984.

I spent two months there learning each area of the floor, from input to output. I started in the stockroom, where they received the raw materials for making pressure gauges. I then moved to preparing raw materials for production. I also did light machine work to press cases out of sheet metal and ended up doing calibration of gauges as the final stage of production. I look back at that time as one when I learned to respect the process, craftsmanship and dedication to the manufacturing craft.

This was the summer that solidified my belief in process as the key to success.

In 1987, I was about to graduate from LSU in industrial technology. I could have easily gone to work for the family business, but felt the need to go out and get a job on my own first. I landed an interview with my dream job at the time, Texas Instruments. This was the big one – the interview everyone on campus wanted. After my trip to Dallas for the interview, I was sure I had the job. My experience with BGI and my summer in Switzerland both seemed to impress the interviewers. But a week later, I received a crushing letter: "Thank you for your interest in Texas Instruments, but …"

Not one to take losing sitting down, I called to ask why. The answer: They were afraid I'd go back to the family business, but added that the area manager had the final say. I called the area manager and pleaded with him to reconsider, assuring him that I didn't have plans to return to the family business. He offered to fly me back to Dallas, and I spent a second full day in what felt like even tougher interviews.

I approached it as if it were an audition. I had to sell myself if I had any chance of getting the job. A week later, I got a letter inviting me to join the team.

I moved to Dallas after spring graduation. As I walked around that first week, I noticed the different colored badges worn by employees: red, blue, yellow, silver and gold. I quickly learned that the badges we wore represented tenure, which determined position in the company. At TI, you started as a red-badge rookie and reported to a blue-badge. Blue reported to yellow, and so on. It was something I was OK with at the time, but I didn't see a long-term future working within this structure as I am big believer in rewards for performance not just tenure.

Ultimately, the interviewers at Texas Instruments were right: I moved back to BGI after it was successful in winning the rights to become the exclusive rep for Yokogawa, a Japanese process control and instrumentation manufacturer. But the experience at Texas Instruments taught me teamwork, hard work and, in the end, who I was and wasn't. I learned that I did not belong in a non-entrepreneurial environment where seniority was a primary driver for advancement.

Applying the Lessons

Despite high expectations from the manufacturer, selling the Yokogawa line was some of the best selling time I have ever had. First, most of our customers had never heard of or experienced the line, so there was no baggage – good or bad – to contend with. Second, Yokogawa made some of the best process control and instrumentation products in the world.

And third, I was still a big believer in solution selling. Our territory, filled with customers in chemical, refinery, pulp and paper, oil and gas, and water and wastewater segments, was ripe for the product offering.

As an outside salesperson, I applied the lessons I learned early on from

Donna in inside sales. As cliché as it might sound, I was truly focused on becoming a problem-solver and not just someone selling product. I wouldn't go in to talk with an engineer, put my product on the table and start reciting the product's features. Donna taught me that the better and more lucrative approach was to build relationships and uncover the problems plaguing a business. I needed to be the solution.

This approach paid off. When I started in full-time outside sales, I was assigned the C and D accounts, what we called the "cats and dogs." They were small accounts for the business. And they certainly had not been priorities in the past.

In addition to approaching these accounts as a problem-solver, I learned to profile them. I would go into a chemical plant, for example, and note the equipment. How many mag meters? Thermometers? Pressure gauges? I'd look not only at what they were using, I'd note the brand and amount. I asked a lot of questions of the engineers and I&E technicians. I started to take detailed notes on paper and eventually transferred them to Lotus Notes. (This was pre-Excel.)

We eventually hired a company to help us plan sales calls and record how many times and how often we called on individual accounts. I decided to take it a step further. I developed significant activity reports (SAR). I would take an account – say, ABC Chemical Company – and list its contacts. Then I tracked the sales calls and touch points I had with each contact at that company. I had a three-ring binder, and every account had its own page. It was the printed version of what we'd put in a spreadsheet today.

I then dove deeper and using codes, started tracking the products I talked with them about. The next step in the process was a more detailed account profile – not just tracking who I talked with and which product was discussed, but also the competition at each account and the volume the account was buying. For example, ABC Chemical has about 100 magmeters in the plant of which 50 percent are Foxboro and 50 percent Rosemount. This information helped me plan and build a strategy on where to spend my time going forward.

Over a couple of months of doing this religiously, I could see where holes existed – who I called on and who I didn't, as well as what I covered in those calls. I was doing that for myself, but I realized these processes could benefit the entire sales team. So I talked with the sales manager at the time, and we incorporated SARs across the company. That helped the salespeople create a visual.

The result: We were selling into places we hadn't before. And our revenue per customer shot up from what might have been a $100-$500 account to a couple of thousand dollars. For C and D accounts, that was a big increase.

As I rose in the ranks of BGI, I also started to incorporate processes around cross-selling into the culture. Customers segregate their suppliers by product category. You need to let them know you have complementary products, or they won't buy them from you. They won't even know you sell them. We used sheets of paper we called "Why Buys." This helped inside sales know why customers should buy an ancillary product from us when they called about product X.

I go back to Donna, our star inside sales team member who didn't just hang up the phone when someone called. The Why Buys automated Donna – albeit fairly manually to start. But these Why Buys also helped train inside salespeople to not hang up the phone. Instead, they asked questions and learned what else was going on with the customer. We also added a Why Buy to any quote we faxed just to plant the seed on other things we could do for the customer. Think about it: If you could expand a sale for one out of 10 calls, what would that do for the bottom line of your company?

My passion for team-selling was also born at this time. At the end of the day, it's nearly impossible for an individual salesperson to be an expert on every line. At BGI, we divisionalized our company. A salesperson was responsible for a handful of products that were complementary, either by industry group or category. Salespeople became experts rather than jacks of all trades. This gave the customers access to category experts and problem-solvers.

Over time, we grew BGI from less than $10 million in annual sales to more than $30 million. Technology certainly played a part in that growth, but a foundation built on a solid and consistent process was the most important factor. And it's a lesson that can be applied across the business.

Process is the key to success, and to get from CRM to ROI, it's all about the process.

Chapter 1
It's About Process,
Not Just Technology

When people think of CRM, they typically think "technology." But this book is about process.

When companies go looking for process improvements, they often throw money at technology with the hope it will do the job. But it's critical to first understand the processes behind the needed change.

Before there was customer relationship management, there was sales force automation. When SFA emerged, there was pushback: How can you automate a sales force? But you're not really automating the sales force; you're automating the processes.

It's time to think differently about CRM. CRM is about managing information within your company to better serve your client or prospect. It helps you:

- Share and leverage touch points in your organization to give you actionable intelligence.

- Better manage leads and opportunities at the front end of the sales process.

When I started down this path in the 90s, CRM was not even an acronym. It was SFA, and before that it was PIM (personal information management) or contact management. And long ago, we used simple Franklin Covey Planners with basic calendaring and task lists. We also integrated wildly important goals, or WIGs, a Covey technique. This involves creating a simple list of what you want to accomplish, ideally with fewer than 10 items, and using that list to drive your battle plan for the week. The idea is to focus on what you can do proactively versus reactively based on customer demands.

Back then, the sales team drove these tools. But the current iteration of CRM has expanded to include more departments. I promote the use of CRM in marketing, inside sales, service and more. It's all about leveraging and sharing the islands of data across your company. Without that, you will not get the ROI you're seeking.

I may have started this journey on paper, but technology has advanced to a point where, with the rise of mobile devices, you don't even need a laptop to log and share this information. Simply pull an application up on your phone or tablet. This has made CRM technologies easier to implement and gain buy-in on. Increasingly, CRM systems are being tied into overall business systems, such as ERP, as well as marketing automation software to link what the marketing team is doing more closely with the sales team's efforts. Business intelligence dashboards allow companies to take the data from their ERP and systems such as CRM and organize and present it in a way that helps them make quicker, better business decisions. This is the Holy Grail for companies. They can take all of the islands of data across departments and put them in one place.

In the past, this was a reality for just large Fortune 1000 companies.

But in the past five to 10 years, we've seen this technology become more affordable and accessible to companies of all sizes. In some ways, however, it's also been commoditized. More vendors offer these solutions, and the technology is growing cheaper. It's become easier to adopt CRM, which makes it even more important to step back and look at how you are using or will use CRM. It also makes it critical to examine which platform you need. How are you ensuring the return on your investment?

Technology Built on Process

The challenge of process-driven technology, rather than tech-driven process, is nothing new. It's something I've been fighting for since the early stages of Selltis, a CRM platform I helped build to automate the processes we had implemented at BGI.

Back at BGI, the leadership team was putting in place a number of new sales processes to support team-selling and other activities so that we could be sure that the right hand knew what the left hand was doing, and vice versa. This was before there was the more sophisticated technology we use today. We tracked the data, but that customer data was not easy to share. The ability to easily share data is one of the biggest shifts we've seen over the years with sales process and technology. It's also an important one.

I wanted to take our significant activity reports and other processes and put them into the hands of our salespeople out in the field. I spotted an opening: A manufacturer had a program where if we met a certain sales number, they would give us an incentive that we could spend on something related to sales. A lot of the companies that received this money spent it on sales training, sales aids and demo equipment. But I wanted to automate the system I had been developing and that, up until this point, had been primarily manual.

I wanted to put laptops in salespeople's hands.

At the time – the early 90s – this was a revolutionary idea, and I met resistance from the manufacturer. I had to sell the manufacturer on the idea that laptops were sales-related. I wanted to put our three-ring binders on those laptops. I wanted salespeople to be able to easily see where gaps existed with companies and contacts, including products they were or weren't promoting – but could be. I wanted to automate the manual processes we had implemented and help the sales team see the value of this.

In the end, we succeeded.

Around the same time, sales force automation was starting to hit my radar. I was excited because it took many of those things I had been manually doing and automated them. It also started to address the front end of the sales cycle, including opportunity management. So I decided to bring in multiple software companies to present how their SFA solutions would help me do what I was looking for. (Think it's hard to get buy-in from employees now? Back then, I struggled to get my father and his partner Charlie Breard on-board. They didn't want to spend the money, but eventually gave me a green light to investigate my options. I think they probably just wanted me out of their office.)

I had five or so SFA companies present their solutions to me. I knew what I wanted from a system, which I think took some of the companies by surprise. I had a detailed specification and wish list. Unfortunately, they came into my office and showed me technology. They didn't understand my business. They only wanted to show off the software engine. And they wanted me to pay them to learn my business, thus taking my knowledge and my vision to build a solution and walk down the street and sell it to someone else.

If someone would have walked into my office with a software solution that was already built and talked the talk and walked the walk of my business, I would probably not be writing this book right now. But I found those five solutions to be generic and not focused on my needs from the industrial sales perspective. If the solutions – and vendors – had been focused on my needs and not just the technology, I wouldn't have had to spend the time and energy to build a solution myself. But in the end, that's what I did.

Thankfully, the presentations weren't a complete loss. One of the companies presented a many-to-many linking solution (a true hyper-relational database) for all categories that you built into the system. This meant you could connect companies, contacts, activity logs, opportunities, projects, expenses, tasks and more. This is exactly what I needed for what I wanted to do. I was introduced to a reseller named Mario Igrec, who would become my partner in what would eventually be called Selltis. We proceeded to build upon the base software to develop a system that could automate the processes I had previously put in place at BGI, including:

- Company and contact management

- Opportunity management

- Target account management

- Project management

- Quoting

- Team selling

- Calendar management

- Vendor visit management

- And more

After working many nights and weekends with Mario over about six months, we implemented Selltis within BGI. At the time, it was just called our sales team process solution.

I quickly learned that other companies in the industrial market were facing the same challenges we were. The first such experience was during a national sales meeting for a manufacturer we represented. During this meeting, I sat next to the CEO of another rep firm and asked if his company had thought about implementing a sales force automation solution. I knew I had struck a nerve, as he quickly answered: "Yes, why do you ask?" I told him we had developed a system internally. He had begun implementing another, but wanted me to show him our homegrown approach.

During my presentation, he tried to find the holes in our system but couldn't. For about an hour, it was like a boxing match on features and functionality. His company was a top-level rep firm in the U.S. and always wanted to be ahead of the curve. Immediately after my demo of our homegrown SFA system, he called his IT lead back in Houston and told him to stop the presses.

I had no intentions of selling our solution at that time. My focus was to solve a problem within BGI and put in place sales processes that would give us a competitive edge and help us better manage the family business. I use the visual of a dog chasing the bus. What is the dog going to do once he catches it? In this case, what was I going to do now that we got an order for a software solution that had no name, no documentation and was not ready for prime time or to be sold and implemented inside another company?

But after making that first sale, I realized we had built something that had been missing in the market. We eventually split Selltis off from BGI.

I live by what Steve Jobs said: "The only way to do great work is to love what you do. If you haven't found it yet, keep looking. Don't settle. As with all matters of the heart, you'll know when you find it."

Not that I didn't love what I was doing at BGI, but I was passionate about taking the solution that Mario and I had built to the market. Helping companies with sales processes and technology was in my heart, and I didn't want to say 20 years down the road, "What if?"

I still believe, more strongly than ever, that there is a need in the market today for process-driven technology, just as there was back in 1999. This is why I am writing this book.

Keep It Simple

One of the best examples of process driving technology was also one of first things we tackled when we developed Selltis: quote and quote automation. I wanted a better picture of what each of our branches were quoting to customers. Our problem was that a customer would call one of our offices for a quote and then call another to see if they could get a lower quote. We had no visibility into what other offices were doing; each branch was an island. The customers knew this and were taking full advantage.

We started adding other functionality and features – all driven by the processes we had developed over the years. Process, not technology, drove us. Other companies who have implemented CRM successfully over the years have learned that same lesson.

"A CRM is a great piece of technology, but is useless without a systematic and standardized process," says Chad Hammerly, business unit manager at Ametek. "The two combined are key to successful sales and territory management. A CRM can do as much or as little as a company would like; ultimately the company will get out of it what the company puts into it."

Branom Instrument Co., a Seattle-based rep/distributor, implemented CRM due to what it calls its lack of customer database management and control. "With our new CRM we fully expect to be able to leverage our customer database to make sure customers are handled correctly and that everyone who deals with a customer is on the same page and increases our close rate on business," says Jeff Baker, general manager.

And ProQuip President Dave Lefley says a CRM system has helped the rep/distribution company manage business better with its suppliers. "We showed them how we were managing our business and what information we tracked and the reports easily accessible in our system. We parted way with a major manufacturer back in 2000, which opened the door for us to pursue and attract some new manufacturers. We were very successful with acquiring some new manufacturers and believe our use of CRM was a major factor in our company being selected as their rep," Lefley says.

CRM is not about the technology itself. And it's not about adding data to a system (though that is an important part of the equation). It's about getting data out so that it can be leveraged to better serve customers, just as these distributors are doing to solve specific challenges within their businesses. CRM doesn't have to be complicated. The technology simply makes us more efficient in translating data to actionable insight.

Keith Rainwater, vice president of operations at Andon Specialties, says CRM has proved to be an effective conduit between his organization's customers, sales force and leadership team. "Without it, an organization is forced to adopt a hope strategy in order to achieve its business objectives," he says. "Within our company, the CRM package delivers great value by consolidating all sales pipeline data in a clear, concise format that can be used to effectively communicate with our sales teams and principals. By doing so, we're able to maintain focus and accountability to our sales process and, ultimately, drive positive business results."

We all live in an era of instant gratification; we are used to and can get information when and where we need it. The question is, how are you using this information? How are you leveraging it? How are you slicing and dicing it to your advantage?

It can be easy to let technology get in the way of better process. It can be easy to get overwhelmed with the options and the data available today. And today's technology sits in stark contrast to what I was trying to do piecemeal with what was essentially barbed wire and duct tape when we first built Selltis in 1999. That said, while not as powerful as today's options, it did whittle the technology to its basics and kept the focus on process.

It's not unusual for me to go into a company and hear a potential client say exactly what I said all those years ago when I was pitched software by multiple companies: "I am going to spend a lot of money. What will I get for it?" It's a fair question. How can you ensure you are getting the return you need to justify your investment?

SalesProcess360 CRM Audit

The answer lies in your approach. In this book, I'll outline a line of attack that I have seen work with rep, distribution and manufacturing companies to get the most from CRM: the SalesProcess360 CRM Audit, which we'll discuss in more detail in Chapter 2.

Step 1: Conduct a thorough Sales Process Review.

Use the Sales Process Review to really think honestly about your sales process from every angle of your business. In this review, you'll analyze not only your outside and inside sales, but also marketing, service, customer service and more. You'll also examine your processes at each stage of the sales cycle, including leads, opportunities, quotes and orders.

Step 2: With those results, perform a Sales Process Gap Analysis.

After your Sales Process Review, you will have a much better understanding of where gaps lie in your organization. In the Sales Process Gap Analysis, you will identify the top three gaps in each of your departments, as well as in each sales cycle stage. This is critical, and you will need to be brutally honest with where your company is and the gaps that are preventing your company's growth.

Step 3: Set up your CRM Roadmap Matrix with gaps you identified.
The purpose of the CRM Roadmap Matrix is to remove the subjective and make it clear what you should focus on first with CRM. You'll better understand the scope, difficulty and impact of each item on your to-do list, and identify low-hanging fruit for immediate ROI. This will add structure and purpose to your plan.

Step 4: Fill in your CRM Phased Roadmap worksheet and get to work!
The CRM Phased Roadmap replaces that long CRM needs/wish list. Use the results of the CRM Roadmap Matrix to prioritize which gaps to tackle first. Your road map will give your team direction and vision with the new system and will reinforce that your business is not just throwing CRM at the wall and hoping something sticks. A phased approach also ensures you won't try to do too much, too soon with CRM, which can sometimes overwhelm companies.

Step 5: To justify your investment, use the CRM ROI Calculator.
After going through the previous steps, you will have what you need to fill in the CRM ROI Calculator, which will estimate the return CRM can provide to your business and help you to justify your investment. We'll walk through this in Chapter 3. You may download your own spreadsheet for calculations at ROIfromCRM.com. You'll find – when CRM is done right – that even an increase of less than 1 percent in annual sales will offset your initial investments in CRM technology.

Takeaways

- To get ROI from CRM, lead with process improvements, not technology.

- CRM is the means not an end. It is a conduit to streamlining your business processes.

- Have passion for making this change in your company. If your team sees that passion, they will follow.

- Don't be overwhelmed by the data available in your system. Today's technology lets you easily parse and deliver what you need to the right people at the right time to make better business decisions.

- Use the SalesProcess360 CRM Audit to systematically identify priorities and build a plan for CRM success in your company.

Chapter 2
SalesProcess360 CRM Audit

It's easy to get overwhelmed by CRM. But CRM is not a four-letter word. The SalesProcess360 CRM Audit is a systematic approach that simplifies the process and helps you to identify what to focus on first, as well as what it will take to get it done.

The SalesProcess360 CRM Audit was developed out of a need I found while working with clients early in their CRM evaluations. I'd ask them to provide their specification lists, and what I'd frequently get back was a long list of features. Nothing on the list would be processes they wanted to improve using CRM.

Some common examples on company specification lists include:

- User-friendly
- Link with Outlook
- Web-based
- Easy and intuitive
- Opportunity manager
- Easy-to-get reports
- Can send broadcast emails
- Lead management
- Mobile capability

These are all great check-off items; make sure the CRM you are looking at has or can do these things. But companies need to dive deeper, which is what the SalesProcess360 CRM Audit was developed for.

Imagine a funnel. The results of the first step of the SalesProcess360 CRM Audit are at the top of the funnel and feed into the second, and so on, until you have a clearly defined plan based on your company's true needs, which emerge at the bottom of the funnel. This ensures you are tackling the areas of your business that will provide the greatest ROI in both the short- and long-term. We'll wrap up the process with an analysis that will provide you with real data that you can present to justify your investment in CRM.

The five steps of the SalesProcess360 CRM Audit are:

1. Sales Process Review

2. Sales Process Gap Analysis

3. CRM Roadmap Matrix

4. CRM Phased Roadmap

5. CRM ROI Calculator (see Chapter 3)

1. Sales Process Review

One of CRM's primary objectives should be to improve and automate the sales process with your team, not just outside salespeople. So many companies that I have worked with over the years focus CRM primarily – if not solely – on the outside salesperson. Companies who do this are missing the boat and ultimately where the ROI is with CRM.

Use the Sales Process Review to review your current processes and identify gaps. These gaps are where focus with improved processes and CRM can bring the ROI you seek. I always start with what I call the SPRQ (Sales Process Review Questionnaire). We use this questionnaire to look for the pain by going through each part of your company, similar to a doctor visit. If the doctor doesn't know where the pain is, he can't treat it. If you don't know where gaps exist in your sales process, you can't fill them.

Trivaco, a distributor of valves and controls based in Kentucky, completed the Sales Process Review and the CRM Roadmap Matrix. "The Sales Process Review and CRM Roadmap helped open my eyes to where we needed help the most," says Trivaco President Benjie Pieper. "As a company we felt the biggest impact we could have on growing sales and meeting long-term growth plans was to have a solid process in place on the front end of sales cycle and a CRM that is structured for our specific business in place to help manage it."

The following Sales Process Review questions can be downloaded in worksheet format at ROIfromCRM.com.

Part I: Company

The goal of this section is to get you thinking about your overall business structure. It's probably more complex than you think, so writing down each of the high-level touch points within the business will help you better visualize it. Remember: CRM is about process, not technology. For maximum ROI, your entire team should have a stake in its success.

- Describe your company in terms of territories, branches, divisions and business units.

- Review your management hierarchy, specifically in sales and territory management.

    » Are outside and inside salespeople teamed up?

    » How many outside salespeople do you have? Inside salespeople?

    » Does inside sales report to a sales manager or to the branch/ operations manager?

- Do you have a service department? What is its focus?

- Do you have product specialists? What is their focus?

- Do you have a separate marketing department? What is its focus?

- What is your salesperson review process? How often and what is the format? Provide an overview of your compensation plan.

- When a new outside salesperson is hired, what does the getting-started program look like?

- When a new inside salesperson is hired, what does the getting-started program look like?

- Do you currently have a CRM system? How is the team using it? What are your expectations?

- Is your ERP or accounting system integrated with your CRM system?

Part II: Outside Sales

Think strictly about your outside sales team – how they report on their activity and how they manage the workload they are assigned. Do you have a feedback loop in place with your salespeople?

- Review all the reports and input and update responsibilities for outside sales. For example, weekly call reports. (Provide details: How often, what format, how are reports being used, etc.?)

- What are the average number of accounts for an outside salesperson?

- Do they have target accounts? Define target account.

- If you are using CRM, what are the expectations for the outside sales team for inputting and maintaining it?

Part III: Inside Sales

When thinking about the role of your inside sales team, how much interaction do they have with your outside salespeople? Do you actually call your inside salespeople "sales" or do you call that team "order entry" or "customer service"? What you call this team says a lot about the philosophy of your company. Answer these questions to better understand how your inside sales team is viewed and used within your company.

- Is the title of inside sales actually inside sales? Or is it customer service? Why?

- How are inside sales documenting their interaction with customers?

- Review all the reports and input and update responsibilities for inside sales.

- What are the methods and processes used by inside sales to communicate with outside sales?

- If you are using CRM, what are the expectations for the inside sales team for inputting and maintaining it?

Part IV: Service

For most companies, the service group is an island. If you have a service team, what is its role in the company? Is there any communication between it and the rest of your team? Use these questions to better understand your service team's role in the business and to uncover potential opportunities to maximize its impact.

- If you have a service team, how do they document their work? Where does this documentation land?

- Does service participate in sales meetings?

- If you are using CRM, what are the expectations for the service team for inputting and maintaining it?

Part V: Marketing

While the link between sales and marketing should be clear, unfortunately in many companies, the communication lines between the two departments are broken. No feedback loop exists on the leads generated by marketing, for example, and very little coordination occurs between the two.

- If you have a marketing person or department, provide an overview of what they focus on and how they work with the sales team.

- Do you do any email marketing campaigns? Other campaigns? Give an overview.

- If using CRM, what are expectations/responsibilities for the marketing team's input and maintaining the system?

Part VI: Lead Management

Getting and qualifying quality leads is one of the most critical parts of the sales process. After all, the leads you put in your sales funnel can increase or decrease the chances for sales success down the line. Unfortunately, most companies are handing over nonqualified leads to the sales team with no follow-up process. Think about how your business handles lead management.

- What are your sources for leads?

- Review the lead input and follow-up process within your company.

Part VII: Opportunity Management

Surprisingly, many companies don't have a clear definition of what an opportunity looks like for their business. Before a potential opportunity gets to the quote stage – when it's already too late – how are you handling and qualifying it within the company to ensure you're not just a third bid? Use these questions to think about how you manage opportunities.

- Are you doing opportunity management?

  » What is your definition of an opportunity?

  » Review the input and management process of the opportunity from start to finish.

Part VIII: Quote Management

Is your business a quoting machine? Or are you careful about the opportunities that move to the quote stage? How do you follow-up with quotes and use the data generated by that to look forward with your business? Use these questions to dive deeper into your quote management process.

- What is the estimated number of quotes done a day by the company? By person?

- Who is responsible for doing quotes?

- Are there standards for what quotes look like?

- Who is responsible for updating and managing quotes?

- How are quotes done and presented to the customer?

- Where are quotes stored?

- What is the follow-up process for quotes? (Who, what and when?)

- Are there a lot of phone and email reply quotes given (quick quotes)?

- What do you think is the percentage of quotes that are formal written quotes versus quick quotes (verbal or quick-reply email)?

Part IX: Reports
Now let's look more closely at how you're currently tracking and sharing information within your company.

- What are the key reports management uses to manage business on a weekly/monthly/quarterly basis? Provide specific examples.

- Do you review the reports the sales team gets from management on a weekly/monthly/quarterly basis?

- Do you receive forecasting reports? How do you get those forecasting reports? Discuss your current process for this.

Part X: Additional Sales Process Questions

- Do you establish and manage sales goals with your sales team?

    » Provide an example in detail of who, what and when.

    » How are these goals determined and what is the monitoring process and system?

- Do you do target account management? If yes, provide an overview.

- Are you doing major project pursuit and management? If yes, provide an overview.

- Do you have any salespeople focused on calling on engineering firms or contractors? If yes, provide an overview.

- If I asked your sales team, both outside and inside, about which top three to five manufacturers they should be spending their time on, would I get a consistent answer across the board?

- Do you measure and monitor activity by key manufacturers and products your company needs to focus on? How?

- How are you handling any reports manufacturers are requiring of you?

- How are you handling manufacturer visits? Write down your process, if you have one.

- Have you established key performance indicators (KPIs)?

    » What are they?

    » How do you measure and monitor them?

- Are you profiling contacts and/or companies? (hierarchy, role, interest by product, applications)

- Are you tracking competitors? Explain.

- Are you tracking successes? Explain.

These questions hopefully got you thinking about what I call whole-team selling. Getting ROI from CRM is not just about how to improve outside sales; it's about looking closely at all of the touch points in your company and improving the processes within those.

2. Sales Process Gap Analysis

What we are going to do now is take each of the sections in the Sales Process Review and write down two to three areas of improvement – or gaps – where you feel you could add focus with improved processes. That is our starting point for where you can get the most out of CRM.

Again, download a worksheet at ROIfromCRM.com.

List your gaps in the following categories. I've included a few examples for the outside and inside sales categories below:

- Company
- Outside Sales
  1. System and process in place to better manage opportunities
  2. Automating call reports
  3. Profiling and managing target accounts
- Inside Sales
  1. Documenting communication with customers and prospects and sharing this with the outside salesperson
  2. System and process to help with quote follow-up
  3. System and process to help manage open activity and track service calls

- Service

- Marketing

- Lead Management

- Opportunity Management

- Quote and Quote Management

- Reporting

- Other Areas

3. CRM Roadmap Matrix

After you have listed all the gaps or areas of improvement in each of the categories, fill out the CRM Roadmap Matrix with each. Add each gap under the "focus" column.

Focus: This is the gap (area of improvement/focus).

Departments needed: Which departments will be needed for this?

Value proposition: What is the value proposition for focusing on this particular gap? Why should you do this?

Obstacles: What are the obstacles or hurdles to improving your process in this area?

Difficulty: How difficult will improving this be? Select high, medium or low.

Impact: What is the overall impact of improving this area of your business? Select high, medium or low.

Internal champion: Who will be the internal champion for this improvement? This is the person ultimately responsible. Assign someone with authority as this person may not be the actual person doing it, but may need to delegate.

Figure 2-1: CRM Roadmap Matrix

Download spreadsheet at ROIfromCRM.com

(H=High, M=Medium, L=Low)

Focus	Departments	Value proposition	Obstacles	Difficulty (fill in)	Impact (fill in)	Matrix (calculated)
Example						
Opportunity management	Outside sales	Better management of the front end of sales cycle	Culture change with outside sales	M	H	MH
Automate call reports	Outside sales	Document where & who we see	Outside sales seeing the value	L	H	LH
Profile & manage target accounts	Outside sales	Make sure we spend time in the right area	Time to get accurate data	H	H	HH
Document communication & touch points	Inside sales	Insight for outside sales	Currently not doing add'l work	M	H	MH
System & process for quote follow up	Inside & outside sales	Increased sales	System & commitment to do it	L	H	LH
Track open activity & service calls	Inside sales	Nothing slips through the cracks	System to automate this	L	H	LH

Actions

Focus	Internal Champion	Major Action Item	Changes in CRM System	By Date	Prioritize focus by:
Opportunity management	Sales manager	Develop criteria for "opportunity"			LH
Automate call reports	Sales manager	ID key information to track			MH
Profile & manage target accounts	Sales manager	ID key information to get & track			MM
Document communication & touch points	Inside or customer service management	System to document all communication (phone calls & emails)			HH ←
System & process for quote follow up	Inside or customer service management	System to track quotes with follow up system			
Track open activity & service calls	Inside or customer service management	System & process to track open activity & service calls			

Focus	Add'l Major Action Items	Add'l Major Action Items	Add'l Major Action Items	By Date
Opportunity management				
Automate call reports				
Profile & manage target accounts				
Document communication & touch points				
System & process for quote follow up				
Track open activity & service calls				

Major action items: What are the major actions that will need to occur to move forward on this initiative? List in order of what needs to happen first, second and so on. Depending on the area of focus, this list could be pretty involved. Don't try to think – document everything that is needed initially; list up to three major action items just to get started.

Changes in CRM system: This can apply whether you have a CRM now or not. List the major functionality you will need in a CRM system to do this. Think outside of the box. CRM systems can often do far more than most companies realize.

After you document the gaps, sort them by difficulty and impact.

For example, an LH is a low difficulty but high impact. These are the low-hanging fruit or the quick wins. Focus on these first. Here is a potential order of priority:

1. LH (low difficulty, high impact)
2. LM (low difficulty, medium impact)
3. MH (medium difficulty, high impact)

Go after the low-hanging fruit that will provide return – the r in ROI.

4. CRM Phased Roadmap

Survey after survey has found that industrial sales organizations are often overwhelmed by the idea of implementing CRM either because of past failures or because they anticipate resistance from their teams. For those companies that do jump in, some move too quickly, trying to do too much, too soon. My advice: Start slow and grow.

A phased approach to implementing CRM, with an eye on key pain points identified in your CRM Roadmap Matrix, can ease implementation and adoption. There's no need to do everything at once; you'll go over-budget, and your team will be overwhelmed. And there's a good chance that the change you seek in your sales organization won't come to pass.

Take Branom Instruments' experience: "One of the main things that helped our company was that we started slow with our CRM, and we grew into it as our business needs developed and we gained more aptitude and understanding of the CRM itself and its various capabilities," says President Jeff Baker. "I would encourage anyone looking at a CRM investment to phase it in over time."

I break onboarding into three phases after initial implementation:

- Implementation: First 30 Days

- Phase 1: 30-60 Days

- Phase 2: 60-90 Days

- Phase 3: 90-180 Days

The first 30-90 days in particular are critical to CRM's eventual success.

A big part of onboarding is determining the areas that you're going to focus on first; that drives how you set up your system. This is the direct result of the work you did on your CRM Roadmap Matrix. Shown in **Figure 2-2** on the next page is an example company's CRM Phased Roadmap. Each phase includes training and software preparation, as well as areas of focus for the business, such as contact management or quote management.

To kickstart your CRM implementation and onboarding, start with the end in mind. Determine what you want to accomplish in the phases outlined above based on your CRM Roadmap Matrix. Make sure you're also focused on the long-term. While it is important to start slow, it's also important to build a foundation for the future. If a CRM vendor or consultant on CRM doesn't help you do that, they are not doing justice to your company.

Include representation from inside sales, marketing, service, management and operations in this process. The more departments involved, the more likely you'll lay the right foundation. Get your team to sign off on your focus for each phase, and then set expectations. What will come out of the onboarding process in each phase for each department?

Figure 2-2: CRM Phased Roadmap

Download spreadsheet at ROIfromCRM.com

First 30 Days — Onboarding/Implementation	Phase 1 (30 to 60 days)	Phase 2 (60 to 90 Days)	Phase 3 (90 to 180 Days)
Implementation management w/champion	Initial user training (how)	Continued user training (how)	Continued user training (how)
System setup & management	Initial user training (why)	Continued user training (why)	Continued user training (why)
Data review, cleanup & import	Management coaching	Management coaching	Management coaching
Reporting & dashboard layout	Professional services (modifications)	Professional services (modifications)	Professional services (modifications)
User set up	User training follow up and Q&A	User training follow up and Q&A	User training follow up and Q&A
Workflow review			IT involvement for integration between ERP & CRM
Review forms & fields for input			
Product/Service/Division/Territory review			

Team Expectations

Phase 1

Outside	Company & contact activity mgmt. (sales visits, email, phone calls)
Outside	Opportunity Management
Inside	Company & contact activity mgmt. (email, phone calls)

Phase 2

All	Calendaring
Outside	Quote mgmt. & follow up
Outside	4 dimensional account profiling
Outside	Proactive opportunity mgmt.
Inside	Quote & quote mgmt.
All	Task Management
Service	Company & contact activity mgmt. (service calls)

Phase 3

IT	ERP Integration
All	Vendor visit mgmt.
Outside	Demo tracking
Service	Service calendaring
All	Project management

For each phase, ask these two questions:

- Does what I'm getting ready to do (the process and systems being put in place) help me share and leverage knowledge across my team? Does it bridge the islands of data in my company?

- Does it allow me to better manage the front end of the sales process?

If you can say yes to both of those questions, that means that what you are putting into place will give you a competitive edge. In Chapter 7, we'll look more closely at what you might want to include for maximum ROI in each phase of your onboarding plan.

Takeaways

- Getting ROI from CRM is not just about outside sales; it's about whole-team selling, looking at all of the touch points in your company and improving the processes within those.

- Don't start with long specifications and wish lists when preparing to invest in CRM. Instead, use the simpler Sales Process Review Questionnaire and CRM Roadmap Matrix to identify what to focus on first and chart a path for your company.

- Go after low-hanging fruit first, those items that rank as low difficulty, high impact (LH) in your CRM Roadmap Matrix.

- One of the biggest mistakes companies make is trying to do everything at once with CRM. Instead, start slow and grow.

- Using your CRM Roadmap Matrix results, select a few areas to focus on in each phase of your CRM implementation and onboarding. Don't move to the next phase until your team feels comfortable in the current one.

Chapter 3
A Revenue Generator, Not a Cost

The final step in the SalesProcess360 CRM Audit is to calculate the potential return you may get from CRM based on the data you've uncovered thus far. With the results from the CRM ROI Calculator, you will be able to justify your investment to either yourself or your managers.

Unfortunately, many industrial distributors, reps and manufacturers tend to view any kind of technology investment as a cost. Part of that stems from the need to budget the investment, which is typically done under the eye of the CFO. But in my experience, it takes an increase of less than 1 percent in annual sales to offset their initial investments in CRM technology.

In other words, technology investments done right will result in sales and profitability growth that goes far beyond the expense. It's time for businesses to start viewing CRM as a revenue generator, and not as a cost.

Consider these areas of low-hanging fruit where CRM can have an immediate impact on your top and bottom lines:

Quote Follow-Up
Very few companies I have spoken with over the years have been confident their quote follow-up is as great as it could be. Simply putting an improved quote follow-up process in place will likely yield an increase in sales. Automating it – letting the system generate a follow-up email three days after the initial quote, for example – would increase the hit rate even more. What would it do for your business if you secured additional business from just one out of every 10 quotes that weren't generating sales before the change?

Leveraging Data from Other Departments

When many companies think ROI from CRM, they look only to outside sales. But what about the other customer touch points in your organization? Inside sales, customer service, marketing and product specialists have incredibly valuable customer information that can be shared and leveraged to generate more sales. If you put together a system that truly and effectively shares and leverages this data, what would that mean to your bottom line?

Figure 3-1: CRM at the Center of Departments

For an inside salesperson, the most important customer in the world is the person on the other end of the phone line. A best practice is to take care of the customer's request, but then take a minute or two to inquire about what else is going on or follow up on past interactions and transactions with everyone in the company who has touched that customer. If the inside salesperson has information from other departments at her fingertips, she can be more proactive: "It looks like our service person was out there last week on a valve repair. Did you get everything you needed on that? Anything else I can help you with?" Or "I see that our salesperson is working with you on XYZ product for this project. Do you need more information on that? Can I send you a spec sheet?" The overall impression left on the customer would be positive, and the opportunities for upselling and cross-selling would improve. Inside sales interacts with customers and prospects 20 times more than an outside salesperson. Leverage these touch points.

Sales Team Turnover

The cost of losing a salesperson is steep. When a salesperson walks away, carrying years of customer history with him, what does that cost your business? How long does it take a new salesperson to get up to speed? A CRM system and process enables your business to document that knowledge so that when someone walks away, you lose less.

ProQuip's Dave Lefley found this to be one of the most valuable parts of CRM for his distribution company. "Having that salesperson's past activity in the CRM was priceless," he says.

With CRM, the replacement has a road map to hit the ground running. Rather than asking a customer to bring the new salesperson up to speed – which doesn't look good – she can come in, on top of her game: "You recently had this service issue. Let's talk about whether that issue has been resolved or whether we need to tackle it from another angle." Or, "I see your previous sales rep was working with you on a pump opportunity. Where does that stand, and what is my next action?" Your customer will be much more impressed with the seamless transition, with service that is uninterrupted. What's more, the faster your new team members get up and running, the faster they start to sell and contribute to growth.

Your Service Team

In most industrial companies, the service group is an island. The team is in the shop or out in the field. The interaction the service team has with the sales team is minimal. That's a big missed opportunity that CRM can help you fix.

Your service team has incredible information from its time spent with your customers. The team goes out and repairs valves, pumps and other critical parts, and sees and hears about the real challenges your customers are facing. They are talking with the people who have their finger on the pulse and to the influencers and possible decision-makers. They can get information from them that a salesperson may not be able to because the customer's guard is down. The customer views that service person as one of them, as someone who tells it like it is and is in the trenches with them.

The information the service person gets should be shared and leveraged with the rest of your team. But most companies aren't taking advantage of that. The salesperson may see that there was a service ticket, but he doesn't have the background information on that job. When a service person asks sales-related questions and then uses a system and process to share that information with the outside and inside sales teams, they can uncover new opportunities to expand business with existing customers – one of the biggest opportunities for growth for any business. Train them to always have their antennae up, looking for opportunities. Make the service team your secret sales weapon.

ROI Calculator

CRM is a revenue generator. I've seen it. I've lived it. It comes down to culture. But for this to be true, you have to be ready as a company to change your culture to prioritize better processes and procedures that allow you to share and leverage knowledge across all the touch points in your organization.

ROI from CRM is not an oxymoron. Let's walk through an exercise that will show this. To download your own spreadsheet for calculations, go to this book's website, ROIfromCRM.com. Use your own company's numbers to see what the ROI could look like for CRM in your business.

Start with the input for the ROI calculator. Note there are more complicated ROI calculators out there, but I tried to make this simpler and more straightforward.

The outlined fields represent inputs.

Annual Sales: What are your company's annual sales?

Avg. GP Margin: What is the average gross profit margin percentage across your business?

Figure 3-2: CRM ROI Calculator

Download spreadsheet at ROIfromCRM.com

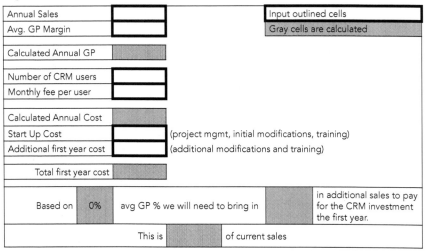

Annual Sales		Input outlined cells
Avg. GP Margin		Gray cells are calculated
Calculated Annual GP		
Number of CRM users		
Monthly fee per user		
Calculated Annual Cost		
Start Up Cost		(project mgmt, initial modifications, training)
Additional first year cost		(additional modifications and training)
Total first year cost		
Based on 0% avg GP % we will need to bring in		in additional sales to pay for the CRM investment the first year.
This is		of current sales

Number of CRM users: How many CRM users will you have on the system? Remember to include departments beyond outside sales.

Monthly fee per user: This is the monthly fee you are paying for each user on the CRM. Most CRM providers offer a subscription-based solution – typically referred to as a SaaS, or software as a service, model – where you pay by the month.

Startup cost: This is your onboarding/implementation cost. The main areas to think about here for the calculation are:

- Project management by the CRM vendor or value-added reseller.

- Importing fees for importing your existing data from Excel, ACT, Outlook, etc., into your CRM.

- Professional service fees for modification/customization of CRM.

- Training cost. Consider onsite, web or both plus travel expenses.

Additional first-year cost: These are typically professional service fees.

The gray fields will immediately calculate based on what you put in.

I have been doing this with different companies for years, and typically increasing current sales less than 1 percent can justify the CRM

A Revenue Generator, Not a Cost

Figure 3-3: CRM ROI Calculator Example

Annual Sales	$20,000,000		Input outlined cells
Avg. GP Margin	20%		Gray cells are calculated
Calculated Annual GP	$4,000,000		
Number of CRM users	20		
Monthly fee per user	$65		
Calculated Annual Cost	$15,600		
Start Up Cost	$10,000	(project mgmt, initial modifications, training)	
Additional first year cost	$3,000	(additional modifications and training)	
Total first year cost	$28,600		

Based on	20%	avg GP % we will need to bring in	$143,000	in additional sales to pay for the CRM investment the first year.
		This is	0.72%	of current sales

investment. Let's look at a real-life example.

A company's annual sales were $20 million with an average gross profit margin of 20 percent. This gave them about $4 million in annual profit. They had 20 CRM users with a per-user monthly fee for the CRM at $65.

This equated to $15,600 in annual fees for the use of the CRM system. The estimated startup cost was $10,000 with an additional $3,000 in modification and training throughout the year. The first-year total estimated cost for the CRM software and onboarding was $28,600.

To pay for this $28,600, the company would need to generate an additional $143,000 in sales based on 20 percent gross profit, which is 0.72 percent of current sales. Less than 1 percent.

An increase in less than 1 percent in sales should be easily achieved based on:

- Focusing on improved sales processes using CRM in the front end of the sales cycle.

- The sharing and leveraging of knowledge that CRM can bring to your team.

Even if you are having a bad year due to circumstances you can't control, such as the economy, instead of being down 10 percent in sales you may only be down 9 percent if you had a system in place that helped you manage the front end of the sales process and effectively allowed your team to share and leverage critical information. Use the 1 percent rule.

Let's dive deeper into some other areas where you can apply some hard numbers to how CRM can make you money.

Figure 3-4: Other Benefits of CRM
Download spreadsheet at ROIfromCRM.com

Areas we can put some numbers to:

1	Increase in sales due to focus & better management of "front end" of sales cycle			1.0%	(increase in % of sales)	
2	Increase in HIT RATE % on quotes generated?	0.5%	Annual $ quoted per year?	$30,000,000		
3	Increase in sales due to better/documented communication between inside & outside sales			1.0%	(increase in % of sales)	
4	Time spent by everyone doing reporting & data crunching per week	4	(# of hrs)		$100	cost per hour
5	Cost of losing a sales rep per year based on the following:					
	$ of lost revenue due to no documented activity for follow up			$20,000	($/yr)	
	Management's time spent with new salesperson trying to get them up to speed on territory due to no road map			$10,000	($/yr)	
	Lost production time of new salesperson during nonsupervised time due to no road map			$10,000	($/yr)	
	Total cost of losing one sales rep			$40,000		
	Average number of sales reps lost per year			1		

These are some very conservative numbers based on the example in **Figure 3-3** for a $20 million-a-year company.

Increase sales through focus and better management of the front end of the sales cycle. You read my belief in 1 percent earlier. I have said to companies that I have worked with over the years that if we can't achieve at least 1 percent in increased sales with a sales-focused CRM approach then shame on us. The front end of the sales cycle includes better management of leads and opportunities. (Read more in Chapter 5.)

A Revenue Generator, Not a Cost

Increase in hit-rate percentage on quotes. This is probably the easiest and lowest-hanging fruit for ROI from CRM. Most companies are quoting machines, but very few companies are follow-up machines. One of my clients told me that before focusing on quote follow-up with its CRM, the company would send quotes to everyone that requested one: "We changed our mindset and put in place a quote qualification process and quote follow-up process. We started to quote less but win more. Our quote hit rate went from an average of 25 percent to more than 35 percent, and we were spending less time doing quotes."

In the example I used a very conservative number of 0.5 percent. Again if we can't achieve a half percent in quote hit rate, then shame on us.

Increased sales due to better communication and documentation between inside and outside sales. In other words, the sharing and leveraging of information and knowledge between two departments. For this example, I used 1 percent. In this example I am not even calculating the other areas possible within your company for sharing and leveraging communication. The big one for companies that have a service department is communication between service and outside sales.

Time spent doing data crunching and reporting. Look at what is really going on at the end of the week, month, quarter and year within your company to get to those reports you need to run your business. It is not bad to have spreadsheets, but you can automate this and not recreate the wheel every week, month or quarter with new and updated information.

An effective CRM will automate those spreadsheets and, even better, result in real-time information. Have a process in place for input into the CRM, and you will get the output you need to run your business.

Cost of losing a salesperson. I have had many owners and vice presidents of sales tell me they can justify CRM based on this cost alone. Consider these three financial impacts:

- *Lost revenue due to no documented activity for follow-up in salesperson's territory if they leave.* If a salesperson leaves for any reason, and you don't have an activity report – and more importantly a pipeline report – on what they were working on by contact, company and product/service, that knowledge has walked out the door in the head of the salesperson. How is your company going to look when the new salesperson walks into an account and has no idea what the previous salesperson was working on with that account? What value can you put on this? In the example, I put $20,000 in lost profit. That is $100,000 in sales that slips through the cracks, probably less than 1 percent of the territory's sales.

- *Management time spent with new salesperson to get them up to speed on a territory with no previous documentation from the salesperson who left.* If there is no road map on the history within a territory of previous activity and pipeline (including sales visits, issues, things being discussed outside the previous sales activity which can be taken from the ERP/accounting system), then what does the new salesperson have to work from? In most cases sales management or a senior salesperson will have to spend additional time with the new salesperson helping them to get up to speed on the history within the territory and trying to figure out where the bodies and land mines are buried. If you had had documentation of that territory, it may have shortened the learning curve. Put a conservative number on what this is worth, and I think you will quickly see what this could be costing you. In **Figure 3-4** I used $10,000, which represents a third of what you need to pay for the first year of CRM with just this alone.

- *Lost production time for a new salesperson during nonsupervised time due to no road map on previous activity.* You have heard the phrases "twiddling your thumbs" and "lost ball in tall grass." Do these bring up a picture in your head of a new salesperson taking over a large territory for your company with no road map or supervision on how to manage and grow the territory when they are on their own? A salesperson has good intentions when he starts his job, but reality sets in when he is left alone during the first 30 days of tackling a new territory with a new company. I can speak from experience, as this mountain becomes taller and taller as the first days and weeks pass. What would documentation with activity and pipeline pursuit do for a new salesperson flying solo in the first 30 days? The salesperson would have some direction, something to go into an account and talk about – something to be proactive on. This productive nonsupervised time has a value on it. I put $10,000, again a conservative number. If a lost salesperson costs your company $100,000/year, that is only 10 percent of his salary.

Figure 3-5: Calculating the Bottom Line *Download spreadsheet at ROIfromCRM.com*

	Summary Year 1	CRM Investment	Calculated $	GP	GP $		
1	Increased sales due to "front end" focus	$28,600	$200,000	20%	$40,000		
2	Increased hit rate on quotes	$28,600	$150,000	20%	$30,000		
3	Increased sales from inside and outside sales	$28,600	$200,000	20%	$40,000		
4	Dollars saved on reporting and data crunching	$28,600	$20,800		$20,800		
5	Cost of losing sales rep and no documentation	$28,600	$40,000		$40,000		
					$170,800 on	$28,600 investment	

The Bottom Line

We all like to go to the bottom line. When you add these five areas of ROI, the bottom line in this example is $170,800 on the $28,600 first-year investment. This sounds like a pretty good deal and one we would all like in any of our personal investments.

A closer look at each area:

1. One percent growth in sales alone gives you $40,000 gross profit on the $28,600 first-year investment.

2. Increased quote hit rate gives you $30,000 on the $28,600 first-year investment. As stated earlier, this is probably the area that can be focused on most easily. Most companies are doing quotes, but most companies are not doing the follow-up like they should. It is not too much of a culture change or extra work to put processes, procedures and visibility on this part of your business.

3. Using the 1 percent rule, documenting and streamlining commu-

nication between inside and outside sales can yield $40,000 gross profit on the $28,600 first-year investment.

4. Automating reporting with a CRM instead of Excel spreadsheets around the office can yield $20,800.

5. The three areas I focused on when you lose a salesperson can add up to $40,000 very quickly. Again I have had a lot of owners and vice presidents of sales justify CRM solely based on losing one salesperson a year alone.

CRM should be looked at as revenue generator rather than a cost. I have talked to so many companies over the years that view CRM as strictly a cost and approach it as a necessary evil. This is not the way to start a CRM project. Management needs to promote CRM as a competitive edge within their companies and be an evangelist on how CRM, if effectively implemented, can bring value to everyone on the team.

Do the CRM ROI Calculator for your company and see what your ROI could be. Download the spreadsheet at ROIfromCRM.com.

Takeaways

- CRM should be viewed as a revenue generator, not a cost to your business.

- To truly get ROI from CRM, you must change the culture to prioritize better processes that allow you to share and leverage knowledge across all touch points in your organization.

- Find ROI from CRM in unexpected places to gain an edge on your competition.

- If you have a service team, make them your secret sales weapon.

Saying Goodbye to Manual

As Steve Molinari became more involved with the sales management of Jensen Instrument Co., he was frustrated with the amount of manual labor, paper orders and reports the business generated. As an outside salesperson, he was required to develop handwritten sales logs, which were never reviewed by the management.

"Inside sales didn't know what outside sales was doing, or vice versa," Molinari says. "Every time we had a salesman change in a territory, the incoming salesman received a handwritten list of companies and customers, which may have been up-to-date or not, if legible." As a result, startup for a new salesperson was slow.

Molinari followed the paper trail from quote to order to invoice to determine how many times each order was touched (and therefore how many opportunities there were for an error). He estimates it was up to 15 times on average.

Now president of Jensen Instrument Co., Molinari recalls Jensen's first attempt at implementing CRM. "It didn't fit our sales process, was cumbersome and too expensive," he says. "Basically we only got a customer and contact list from this effort, but it was a start."

The process instrumentation and controls distributor shifted to a CRM solution developed for the industry. "Our implementation target was to use our CRM for all presales activity, and it was accomplished," he says. "Our timing was perfect as we downsized from five salesmen to two, due to principal changes and market changes in our area. Being lean and mean meant we really needed to be time-conscious and well-documented. We could now easily track projects, opportunities, quotations and correspondences."

Lessons Molinari learned include:

- CRM can't be used as a micromanagement tool, or your team won't use it.

- CRM is only as good as the information entered into it.

- Make sure only necessary information is added. Timely valid information should be the goal.

"It is difficult to quantify a monetary value of a CRM, but I know we could not perform the volume of work we do, with the amount of employees we have without it," he says. "I figure you would have to have two to three employees entering, tracking and developing reports to manage what we manage with our CRM."

Chapter 4
Why CRM Succeeds or Fails (It's Up to You)

Even if you are sold on the value that CRM can bring to your company, there are several obstacles to clear to get the ROI you're looking for.

Viewing CRM as just technology is a common reason CRM fails. Sure, technology is at CRM's core, but it should never be the lead. I will repeat this again and again. Think of CRM as a process, a system for sharing and leveraging your team's data and knowledge. Technology helps you to automate that system and manage the sales process from lead to close and beyond.

Despite the clear benefits, we estimate only about 20 percent of industrial companies perceive they are getting the ROI they were looking for from CRM. The reasons why fall into four buckets: expectations, data, management and culture.

Expectations

High Expectations

Many companies expect that CRM will be a silver bullet. CRM will solve all of their sales woes and will do so quickly. Many also believe that the change will come easily. But it probably won't. CRM is work. You cannot just install software and expect everything will fall smoothly into place. Planning for the shift is critical, and that includes ongoing training to ensure that your team is using and taking full advantage of the benefits that CRM can bring your company.

You must also understand from the get-go the expectations your team has by department, from outside and inside sales, to the service and marketing teams. For example, I see salespeople frequently just along for the ride; they aren't brought into the equation until the end of the process – a big mistake.

Not Understanding Total Cost of Ownership

Companies frequently don't understand the true total cost of ownership (TCO) of a new CRM system. Total cost can be up to four times to seven times that of the software itself, depending on the functionality you are rolling out to the team. When companies underestimate the cost to implement CRM correctly, they are frustrated when expectations do not align with reality.

Think of TCO as an iceberg: The initial cost of the system is the iceberg poking out above the water. For actual icebergs, that tip represents just 10 percent. But a lot more remains under the surface. To effectively implement CRM, you must invest the time and money to reap the ROI that you want. This may include modifications to meet specific needs in your company. It definitely includes training, which should be a priority before, during and after implementation. It is not a one-time event.

If your eyes are just on the initial cost, you'll see the tip of the iceberg but you'll miss what's underneath. CRM vendors are frequently viewed as the bad guys when the ROI goal is not hit. But frequently, the company didn't step up to the plate with the time, money and commitment to make the change. CRM should be viewed as a long-term strategy – not a one-time project.

The Wrong CRM Vendor

CRM requires more than a one-and-done approach. Companies that view a CRM provider's job as complete after the software is installed often find that the real challenges start after implementation. That's why you should view your CRM provider as a partner. You'll be tied to them for the life of the technology, so ensure they are bringing added value to the table. Also be sure they've worked with companies in your industry before. Don't forget to ask for references. Many vendors will overpromise; keep your expectations in check. (Read more in Chapter 9.)

Data

Bad Data

Data – including contacts, email addresses, phone numbers, customer history and more – is frequently a major speed bump for companies on the road to successfully implementing CRM. Many companies feel they have good data, but when they peel back the onion, they find more to clean and update than they expect. If you're not sure about your data, don't bring it into the new system. Rather than struggling with bad data for the life of the CRM, start from scratch. In three to six months, you will have far better confidence that the data you are acting on is reliable.

Islands of Data

For CRM to succeed, it has to be used to leverage data from all customer-facing touch points in your company. Unfortunately, islands of data exist throughout your business, and they aren't usually in sync. Outside sales may maintain a spreadsheet (or several) and their own Outlook contacts, while another repository of data sits with the service department. Customer service and inside sales may manage additional troves of data in the ERP system, which typically outside sales does not have the keys to. All of this data lives in different systems. What's more, your departments aren't sharing this valuable information. These resources offer a huge opportunity for companies that can bring them together under one umbrella and implement processes for a team approach to CRM for maximum ROI. If you don't prioritize this, you'll miss out on at least half the return on your CRM investment.

Double-Dipping

I've seen companies implement CRM, but behind the scenes, its sales team and other employees are still using spreadsheets as their security blankets. They're double-dipping and putting data in two places. And in many cases, the CRM system becomes a very high-priced Rolodex for contacts, while the sales pipeline is really still managed in Excel spreadsheets. The sooner you cut the cord, the better.

Management
Murky Vision
Mixed signals from senior management can have a big effect on CRM's success. In some cases, management is completely missing in action. They had to be involved to approve the project and work it into the budget, but after the approval, they disappear. In other cases, employees may simply view the CRM project as just another management fad. They don't invest in its success because they expect management to move to the next great thing in short order.

The team has to see that CRM will be a part of the culture and strategy going forward. Employees need to see that senior management is engaged and that their involvement goes beyond approval. Managers need to be involved in strategy meetings and must set a vision for what CRM can do to get the company from point A to point B to grow the business. Their role is to make sure that the project stays on course, set expectations and reinforce those expectations constantly.

Culture
Culture is the most important contributor to a CRM's failure or success. If key players are resistant to change, it can be a cancer to your organization. If culture is standing in your way, you'd have a better chance of succeeding if you took the money you invested in CRM to a local casino. Despite the challenge, it can be done. I tell managers all the time: If you are not ready to change the way your company does things, don't do this right now.

Doing Too Much Too Soon
Don't cram too much into the start of the implementation. If you do too much too soon, you risk overwhelming and confusing your team. Instead, pick a handful of items you want to focus on for improvement in your sales process. Areas of focus may include opportunity management, lead management or complaint tracking. Start slowly and build on each success. The SalesProcess360 CRM Roadmap Matrix involves selecting an area of focus, determining which departments are affected, why a change is needed, any obstacles that could stand in your way, the

difficulty and impact of the change, internal champions and the major action items to accomplish the change. It's a simple and powerful process that takes the emotion out and allows you to build on a solid foundation. (Read more in Chapters 2 and 7.)

Start slow and grow.

What's In It for Them

The sooner you can get the different stakeholders in your organization involved in the CRM implementation, the better. When I say stakeholder, I am referring to your entire team, everyone who touches customers and has a need to communicate internally. Get a representative from each department involved early in the process of evaluating CRM vendors and areas of focus, including inside sales, outside sales, service, marketing, specialists, engineering, management and others. Map out expectations and work with them to understand what's in it for them.

At the end of the day, you have to view this process through their eyes. What will motivate them to fully participate? Why should a salesperson take the time to log a sales opportunity, link it to a product code in the system and add a close date? The sales manager benefits because he can then provide a more complete report to the manufacturer, who may want a forecast for the next quarter, but what's the benefit for the salesperson? Beyond just doing her job, how will logging that information help her perform better?

Another example: How does the participation of inside sales benefit the outside sales team? If an inside salesperson logs a complaint, the outside salesperson on that account will not be blindsided by it the next time he visits that account. Everyone must understand the big picture and look at it from the overall company perspective of supporting the client and growing the business.

This comes back to having a strong management team that is an evangelist for the process and system.

No Internal Champions

Without project champions, you'll struggle to gain buy-in from the entire team. Ideally, you'd have a champion from every department that will use the tool, as well as a champion at the management level. Select a successful and respected salesperson who has been with your company for a long time. Make sure everyone in the company knows who those champions are. Tap an overall champion for the project who has veto rights if the team can't make a decision. Typically that is a senior manager involved in the meetings. The more structured your implementation team, the more likely you will succeed.

No Top Gun Involvement

Getting your top guns on your sales team involved from the beginning is critical. The top guns are those salespeople who have been working for you for a long time; they are good at what they do, and they have the respect of their teammates. Getting them involved early on will pull other people into the project. When you tap your top guns to play a part in leading the transition, tell them how critical their roles are. Stress that their buy-in will help make the CRM project a success.

Your top guns should not dominate the team, but they will play a critical role on the cross-functional team that will evaluate and analyze what your business needs from CRM and which areas CRM will target first for improvement. If your top guns are not involved, they can hurt the chances for success. Balance the perspectives of your seasoned top guns with ideas from newer employees to provide a fresh point of view on the process. Your cross-functional team will need a balance of leaders and followers, as well as levels of seniority and departments.

Staying in the Comfort Zone

Recognize that in the beginning the transition will be painful. Your team will want to revert to comfort zones: Excel spreadsheets, sticky notes, notepads, Access and other security blankets. This can result in a slow death for CRM. We are all creatures of habit, and breaking out of those habits is not easy. If your company is not truly ready for change, don't pull the trigger. But if you are ready, drive the change and set a new course for your business.

Not Positioned as a Team Solution

CRM has to be positioned as a team solution. This means leveraging knowledge among all the touch points in your company – not just within your sales team. If you only look at CRM as a sales solution, you will not reap the full benefit of your investment. In fact, you are missing more than half the value of CRM for your business. This mindset needs to start long before the day of implementation. If you want to run a pilot on a new system, for example, insist on including more than your outside salespeople. The goal should be taking the islands of data in your organization and putting them in the same place. If you're not ready for that, then you should wait to move forward with CRM. (Read more in Chapter 7.)

Handing the Project Over to IT

Many companies position CRM as a software implementation project and immediately turn it over to the IT team to manage. This is a mistake and should serve as a red flag. Sales management doesn't get involved like it needs to. But for a greater chance of success, CRM needs to be viewed and managed as a sales solution and approached with process front of mind.

Certainly, IT needs to be involved. Without question, it is a key component of the process. But when it's perceived as a team sales solution versus just software, it shifts the mindset of those you're asking to make such a significant change. Again, CRM is about process, not technology. I believe so strongly in this that if a company hands a project directly to the IT team, I will sometimes bow out because I ultimately know where it will end up.

Limited Training

Investing in training is a critical piece of getting the ROI you need from a system. Turning training over to a technical person, training users on the "how" of CRM, patting them on the back and saying "Go get 'em" will not give you the results you seek. Over time, your team will have questions; if you don't provide a platform for them to get answers, they will revert back to their comfort zones.

The cost of training is minimal, but it is one of the most valuable things you can do to ensure the overall success of your CRM implementation. The first 30 to 60 days are critical to your success. Train your team not only on the How, but on the Why. Especially in the beginning, your team needs to see and understand the big picture, as well what's in it for them. (Read more in Chapter 8.)

Takeaways

- Don't move forward with CRM if you are not ready to change and commit to spending the time and money to make this a success. Culture is the No. 1 reason CRM initiatives don't succeed.

- Don't let what's under the iceberg sink your CRM initiative.

- Involve your entire team before, during and after CRM implementation.

- View CRM as an integral part of the way you do business, not as a one-time project.

- While the IT department should be involved, it should not lead your CRM project.

Chapter 5

ROI Starts with the Front End of the Sales Process

The pursuit of sales is like going into battle. Most companies go into battle relying on past successes with their people, products, services and experience. But it's time to go to battle with some new weapons.

In the past 20 years, I've run into far too many companies who are managing their businesses from the back end of the sales cycle. I understand this. At the beginning of my industrial sales career, I, too, was guilty of focusing primarily on the back end. But for true competitive edge, the place to start is the front end of the sales cycle. Managing the front end of the sales cycle is core to this and a prerequisite for most of what I talk about in this book.

An effective CRM system will help you to better manage the front end, giving you the structure you need to manage from lead to order, which is critical if you want to reap the rewards. And who doesn't? That's why you are reading this book.

But remember, process – not technology – will get you there. CRM will help you automate and improve processes, but it's up to you to understand and implement the fundamentals that will take your business to the next level.

Imagine the sales process in the 360 degrees of a circle. The back end is the quote-to-order stage. The front end includes leads and opportunities, the 180 degrees that companies tend to dedicate fewer resources to.

Figure 5-1: 360-Degree View of Sales Cycle

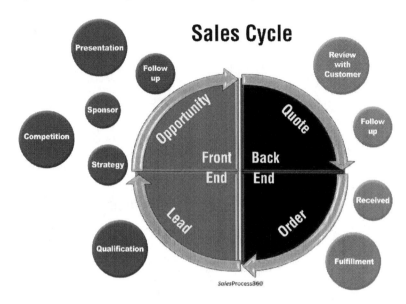

If we look at this linearly, the major areas of the sales cycle look like this:

Figure 5-2: Linear View of Sales Cycle

The most critical point in the pursuit of sales is between the opportunity and quote stages, or between the front and back ends of the sales cycle. This is where the sales are won. Weaknesses in process and management at this critical juncture will put you on the outside looking in.

When you complete the SalesProcess360 CRM Audit, you will likely uncover your company's own weaknesses on the front end of the sales process. This is common. Many industrial companies fall short on the front end. Why? The answer lies in the past. Many companies struggle to break old habits. We all naturally resist change, and this change is particularly difficult.

Let's step back and walk through each component of the front end of the sales process.

Lead Stage

This is the start of the sales cycle. A lead includes potential customers that have shown a level of interest in your products and services. The key word here is interest. At this stage, a lead has not been qualified as a real opportunity yet. Frequently, leads come from trade shows, someone inquiring for information from your website or something you hear out in the field. I also see many companies classify a lead as just a contact who may have some interest in your company's offerings. They may also refer to them as prospects. I like to classify a lead as a contact interested in a particular product or service. For example, a contact may have multiple leads linked to him. He went to a trade show and was interested in one of your products. The following week he sent in an inquiry via the web about another one of your products.

Think about how you handle the following. Score your company on each part of the lead stage from 1 to 5, with 5 being excellent and 1 being poor:

1. Lead generation: Do you have a system for generating leads? There are many options, including your website, trade shows or email campaigns. If you work with your manufacturers to generate leads, where do those leads originate?

2. Lead qualification: A qualified lead represents someone who has shown real interest in your products and services. Not every lead that you generate will fall under this category. For example, a manufacturer may hand you a list of leads from a pile of business cards collected in a drawing at a trade show. Those names represent people who wanted the chance to win an iPad, not necessarily those who showed interest in the booth's contents. This is why it is important to sort the qualified from the unqualified.

When a lead comes through the door, how do you qualify it? Is it simply forwarded to a salesperson? If there is no qualification process in place, no one is qualifying the lead. And because the salesperson is working on other qualified opportunities and following up on existing quotes, those leads frequently are left untouched, meaning that when the salesperson does get around to it, it may already be too late to cash in on that potential opportunity.

Companies that effectively manage leads have processes in place to qualify leads before they even get to the salesperson. They have established the questions they need to ask before leads move to the next stage of the sales cycle. For example:

- Why is the person inquiring about your products or services?

- How did they find out about your company and products?

- Is there an approved project or funds for your products or services?

The sales team needs to know that the company is spending time and resources to qualify the lead, rather than just forwarding every lead and expecting the sales team to take it to the next level.

3. Lead follow-up: Are there follow-up procedures for qualified leads? Is there a system to document the information you get? If the lead has been qualified and turned over to the sales team, how are you ensuring the sales team is following up on the leads by closing them or moving them to the opportunity stage? This is an incredibly important part of sales management.

If leads are being qualified, but the sales team is not converting them to the opportunity stage, review your process and figure out where the problem or miscommunication lies. Is it a lack of follow-up from sales or are you asking the wrong questions at the qualification stage?

Here is a simple scorecard to see how your company stacks up at this stage.

Lead Generation	
Lead Qualification	
Lead Follow-up	
Average Score	

Bottom line: Most companies average a score of 1 and 2 at the lead stage. Companies often get leads and forward to the sales team with no system to track and manage. They put the responsibility on the sales team to qualify them and depend on hope that the sales team moves that lead to the opportunity stage. But hope is not an effective strategy. A system that ensures quality at the front end – with qualified leads – will improve the results you see on the back end.

Opportunity Stage

The next stage we want to look at is the opportunity stage. An opportunity is not a rumor. It is something that has been qualified and has a real potential to move to the quote stage and, ultimately, turns into an order.

Grade your company on the following actions:

1. Opportunity management system: Do you have a system to manage opportunities? Are you tracking key metrics for those opportunities? These include expected close date, the next strategic action that needs to be taken, competition for those opportunities, etc.

2. Standards to define an opportunity: Does your sales team know the criteria for an opportunity? Do you know if the opportunities being chased are good opportunities? Not all opportunities are good opportunities.

3. Proactive follow-up: Do you have a system to track follow-up on your opportunities? Are you tracking the reasons you won or lost opportunities?

4. Reporting: Do you have an accurate opportunity pipeline report? Do you know your percent conversion from opportunity to quote? Can you quickly and easily get a 60/90/120-day forecast? With what level of confidence?

Here is a simple scorecard to see how your company stacks up at this stage. Remember: 5 is excellent and 1 is poor for each of the following:

Opportunity management process and system	
Standards for defining an opportunity	
Proactive follow-up process and team accountability	
Accurate reports in the hands of both the sales team and management	
Average score	

The bottom line: The opportunity stage is probably the most important for growing your business, but often it is not effectively managed. On average, companies will grade themselves around 2 or 3 at this stage. When you really focus on this stage of the sales cycle, you will find a pot of gold at the end of the sales rainbow. If you are just managing your business at the quote stage, you are not in control; in most cases, your competitor is driving. Specifications are written at the opportunity stage. The time between opportunities and quoting is the most critical time in the sales cycle. Is your product or service being spec'd in? Or is it your competitors'?

The Ws: Moving Opportunities Forward
Another area I focus on is what I call the Ws. The Ws are questions that salespeople should be asking the customer when they are working opportunities to further qualify them.

Here are the opportunity stage Ws:

- **Who is on the decision team?**
  Answering this helps you determine whether you are covering your bases by interacting with the right people at the customer. (For example, user buyer, technical buyer, economic buyer, etc.)

- **Who else is being considered as a potential vendor?**
  Knowing your competition can help you position your product or service more effectively.

- **What is the reason you want to purchase this product or service?**
  Let the customer know you want to understand the need and application to ensure you are offering the correct solution and not just selling a product.

- **When will you need a formal proposal?**
  This will tell you where the customer is in the buying cycle and whether it matches where you think it is in your sales cycle. You may think the customer is at the opportunity stage when in reality it is still at the lead stage or very beginning of the opportunity stage.

- **What is the decision process?**
  This will tell you again whether you are interacting with the right people and where they are in the buying cycle.

Incorporate these questions into the opportunity form within your CRM system. Keep these questions in front of the sales team and make them answer them on the opportunity form so that you know they have covered their bases. This also ensures you stay on the same page as they move the opportunity through the sales process. I have had sales managers tell me that just by adding and requiring their sales teams to answer these Ws on the opportunity form, their sales teams' training is reinforced.

Monitoring the Opportunity Process
I challenge you to really look at the data your sales team is adding to your CRM at the opportunity stage. Start looking at the trends. Create a simple scorecard. Keep your eye on opportunity input trend by: company, salesperson, key products/services, territory, division by both dollars and number of:

- Open opportunities

- Overdue opportunities
- Forecast/pipeline

The following example can serve as a scorecard for the overall company, salesperson, key products/services, territory and/or division.

Figure 5-3: Opportunities Sample Scorecard

Opps		Load Input Goals	Jun	Jul	Aug	Sep	Oct	Nov	Dec
		Month #							
		Month Total $							
		Total Open #							
		Total Open $							
		Overdue #							
		Overdue $							
		Forecast							

Managing your business more effectively at the opportunity stage is your leading indicator for your business. (Read more in Chapter 6.)

Quote Stage

The next stage on our journey is the quote. Again, grade your company on a five-point scale for the following actions:

1. Quote generation: Do you have standards for what a quote looks like, how to quote and where to document the quote? When Company A receives a quote from your company, does it look the same as the quote it received from another person in your company? If your answer is no, then your grade on this will be lower. In our family's sales company, this was the case when I started. Someone at a customer could call and ask for a quote for pressure gauges and an inside salesperson would generate the quote using his own format; the next day another inside salesperson would quote the customer in a different format. That's not even looking at whether the customer was quoted the same price or given the same discount for the same product.

2. Quote retrieval: Do you have a process to organize and store all the quotes generated in your company? Can you quickly access all open quotes for a customer? Do you know how many quotes were completed this week, last month and last year?

3. Quote follow-up: How are you following up on quotes? Do you have a proactive process in place? Does your team (outside and inside sales) know who is responsible for following up on quotes?

4. Reporting: How quickly can you get a report on current open quotes? How accurate would that report be? Do you know your quote hit rate (won/lost)?

Here is a simple scorecard to see how your company stacks up at this stage. Use the same scoring standard as before: 1 to 5, with 5 being excellent and 1 being poor.

Qualification questions to determine whether you should even quote	
Standards for what the quote says and looks like	
Quote log on what has been quoted and to whom	
Quote follow-up system (Is it up to date?)	
Reporting system in place for quote activity	
Average score	

The bottom line: Most companies average about 3 to 4 on the quote stage of the sales cycle. Some do a little better than others on quote generation and standards, but many fall short on the follow-up. If a prospect has reached out for a quote, and you have done the work to put the quote together, following up should be easy.

Some companies tend to be quoting machines. But are they order-getting machines? This might go against the grain of sales, but I have coached and consulted companies and seen improved results – higher hit rates, less wasted time and increased sales – by putting every request for quote through a process to determine if that RFQ was worth quoting in the first place.

Don't become the customer's source for a third bid. After all, quoting equals time and money.

Here are some things to consider when asked to quote:

- Have we done business with this company before? (If the answer is no, you might want to reconsider or have strong answers for the following questions.)

- Has this company purchased this product/service before?

- Have we been working with the technical and user buyer on this RFQ? (Was there an opportunity we have been working/tracking for this RFQ? Or did it just land on our desk to quote?)

- Is my product spec'd in, or is my competitor's spec'd in?

- Are they using me as a third bid? What is our track record over the past six to 12 months of quoting this customer? Have we quoted them 10 times with no resulting orders?

Quote Stage Ws

- **What is the return for doing this?**
  You may have asked this question back at the opportunity stage, but at this stage you are probably dealing with a different lead person (for example, purchasing). This might also help you position total cost of ownership (TCO) for your product or service.

- **What is your budget, and has it been approved?**
  This question confirms the client's buying cycle is in line with your perception of where you are in the sales cycle.

- **Who else are you expecting quotes from?**
  Position your value proposition around your knowledge of these competitors and make sure you are highlighting your strengths. For example, if you know you are quoting against Manufacturer X and that manufacturer has been experiencing long delivery times, promote your quick delivery and how much that will save the company.

- **When are you looking at releasing the purchase order?**
  This also confirms the buying cycle and the client's perceived place in your sales cycle.

- **What is my next action, and when?**
  When asking this question, just ask and listen. The client's reply can tell you a lot.

- **At the end of the quote process: Why did I win/lose?**
  If you lose, take the opportunity to find out why so you can learn from it. Tell the customer you really want to understand what you could do differently next time. Make sure you document this in your CRM so that information can leveraged next time around.

Add these questions to your quote form or log for each quote in your CRM system. Keep these W questions in front of both the inside and outside sales teams; inside sales teams most frequently generate the quotes.

I challenge you to really look at your quote process and quote pipeline. Look for trends. Create a simple scorecard. Keep your eye on:

- Quote input trend by: company, salesperson, key products/ services, territory, division

- Overdue quotes

- Quote forecast

- Won/lost quotes

- Reasons won/lost quotes

- The example can serve as a scorecard for your company, salesperson, key products/services, territory and/or division.

Figure 5-4: Quotes Sample Scorecard

Quotes	Load Input Goals		Jun	Jul	Aug	Sep	Oct	Nov	Dec
		Month #							
		Month Total $							
		Total Open #							
		Total Open $							
		Overdue #							
		Overdue $							
		Won							
		Forecast							

When you have compiled three months of data into the scorecard, it will be obvious where you need to focus. For the purpose of the scorecard above, use the load input goal column to create goals. (This will be discussed in detail in the next chapter.) If the monthly number is greater than the goal, put that number in green; if the monthly number is less than the goal, put it in red. Select a range – for example, 20 percent – and if the result falls within that range, put it in black.

Order Stage

Companies typically do best on the order stage and rightfully so. I don't think I have ever talked to a company that did not have processes and procedures for entering and managing orders.

Grade your company on the following actions on the same five-point scale used before:

1. Order write-up standards: Does your company have standards for how orders are written up? Most companies I work with can score themselves with 5s on this part of the order stage. If you don't have a standardized process for orders, you will probably be out of business soon.

2. Order retrieval: Does your company have an order retrieval system? Can you put your hands quickly and easily on orders and the statuses of orders? I typically find 4s and 5s for this specific area, as well.

3. Payment follow-up: How do you handle overdue payments for orders? Most companies have a system in place for this.

4. Reporting: Can you easily get the back-end reports you need? How many orders or payments are 30/60/90 days old? Most companies are usually able to rank this category with 4s or 5s, as well.

Here is a simple scorecard to see how your company stacks up at this stage.

Order-writing standards	
Order retrieval system	
Payment follow-up system	
Ease of retrieving order status reports	
Average score	

The bottom line: Most companies average between 4 and 5 on all of the categories in the order stage. This is how you stay in business, get orders, process orders, get payments and pay your team. It does require some of your focus, but there are other areas that need as much if not more of your focus to grow your business.

How You Stacked Up

So how did you do? Were your back-end numbers higher than your front-end numbers? If so, the good news is that you now have an opportunity to focus on the most critical phase of the sales process to gain that competitive edge.

I typically see these scores when asking companies to share their results:

- Lead Stage: 1 and 2
- Opportunity Stage: 2
- Quote Stage: 3 and 4
- Order Stage: 4 and 5

After the first pass, take the time to document each step of your company's existing processes from lead to opportunity to quote to order. Then, do the exercise again and see if you come up with same score. With this documented focus on your front end, you can now critically review and evaluate your methodology: Where are the gaps, inefficiencies and lack of visibility on the front end? Get your team involved with this review, as well. Make sure they see this and have bought into the need for process improvements in each of these stages. Getting them involved early will pay off down the road when you start to focus on this and make the needed changes within your company.

The Back End Matters Too

I don't want you to walk away from this chapter thinking I believe the back end of the sales process is unimportant. It is very important. But most companies have already put processes, procedures and visibility at this stage. The purpose of this exercise has been to get you to think about how your company is managing the early, critical stages of the sales process. Managing the sales cycle does not have to be complicated. Put equal emphasis on processes, procedures and visibility at all stages of the sales cycle. Don't neglect the front end. This is where you can separate yourself from your competitors.

I have experience firsthand what focusing on the front end can do for a company. This is where CRM shines. Technology used to automate effective processes and procedures on the front end is a big area for ROI from CRM.

Takeaways

- Managing the front end of the sales process is one of the biggest opportunities to get ROI from CRM.

- Aim for scores of 4 and 5 in the lead, opportunity and quote stages.

- Raising your scores on the front end of the sales process will require commitment across your business.

- If your company is not ready to change and put processes in place to better manage the front end of the sales cycle, don't spend the time and money on CRM. You will not get the ROI you are seeking.

A Team-Selling Philosophy

JCI Industries has three or four people touching a sales opportunity at any given time. "It's important that they work together through that process," says Chip Toth, president of the industrial and wastewater equipment distributor, which has a heavy emphasis on service and application.

About 15 years ago, JCI Industries adopted CRM as a tool to do just that. "It doesn't matter if it's the inside person, the outside person, a specialist or someone in the shop, the more information you have, the better you have a chance of landing the order," he says.

And the better that information, the more useful CRM can be. JCI adopted a philosophy of ensuring a quote or opportunity is qualified before moving forward. "You really need to understand what your customer is looking for before you quote it," he says.

Toth believes strongly in focusing on the front end of the sales process. "A lot of people spend a lot of time on the back end of the process. That's like reading the sports page after the game is over," Toth says. Instead, a focus on the front end means a focus on how to win the order – not just analyzing it after the fact. "If you don't have a handle on the front end of the system, you really don't have a handle on your business," Toth says.

For JCI, CRM has become a way of life. "This is what we do every day," he says. "(CRM) is not something where you put it in, and then you leave it alone and it's done. It's a way of doing business."

Chapter 6
Your Leading Indicators

When you embark on your CRM journey, take advantage of CRM's automatic reporting on your team's progress toward your goals. Your CRM Roadmap Matrix and Phased Roadmap will direct you on your first steps, but to ensure ongoing success, identify and track key performance indicators and adjust your direction as needed.

Load Input Goals

If you watch any national news channel, you'll hear about leading indicators. In most cases, the reporters are referring to leading indicators for the economy. Economists track leading indicators such as the Purchasing Managers Index, durable goods orders and consumer sentiment, which tell them where the economy is heading. Every company should have its own leading indicators to better manage the business and understand the direction it is heading.

What is your company's leading indicator? Here are some of the answers I've heard:

- Number of RFQs (request for quotes)

- How my clients are doing

- My sales pipeline

- My bookings against sales goals

Most companies track sales or bookings against sales goals, which is essentially the back end of the sales cycle. This is looking backward. At the front end, tracking your load input against your load input goals will provide you with the leading indicator you need to look forward in your business. Most companies have established sales goals by company, salesperson, territory, product, industry and so on. But most companies have not scratched the surface of load input goals.

This is where CRM can help.

What is load input? And what are load input goals?

Load input is comprised of the new opportunities on the front end of the sales cycle that your company has identified for a set period of time. I like to break this down in months. For example, your new load input for the month of January was $250,000. That means your sales team identified $250,000 worth of new opportunities that month. How do you measure whether this will ultimately get you to your sales goal?

Earlier I said that a common answer to my question: "What is your leading indicator?" is "My sales pipeline." You may argue that a sales pipeline is load input, but sales pipeline is usually just a snapshot of the total number of open opportunities. So the sales pipeline is the cumulative sum of your load input. For example, your sales pipeline is $1 million. That means you have $1 million of potential business in your pipeline scheduled to close sometime in the future.

That may sound really good and may be viewed as a good leading indicator, but what if that pipeline is made up of mostly old opportunities that were identified eight to 12 months ago? Does that pipeline number give you a good indicator for what has been really happening or what is to come?

Managing your load input against your load input goal is a way to take action early in the process rather than waiting until the end of the quarter – or even worse the end of the year – to find out your sales goals weren't met. If goals are missed, the standard retort is: "I'll make it up next month." But this is a reactive rather than proactive way of looking at things.

Load input goal management is a different way to think about and run your business. This concept is about understanding what you need to reach your sales goals in the form of load input, opportunities and/or quotes. It is forward-thinking and proactive rather than based on historic results. It is, in fact, a leading indicator for future business.

Secret Sales Formula:
Sales Goal = Base Business + (New Load Input X Hit Rate)

- **Sales goal** = the annual sales goal for company, salesperson, territory, product, etc.

- **Base business** = the recurring base business built over time for that subdivision, typically MRO business and not including one-time large projects.

- **New load input** = the new opportunities your sales team has identified and is currently working on.

- **Hit rate** = the close-rate percentage your company has experienced for opportunities and quotes converting to orders.

This simple formula will help you get your arms around what your load input needs to be to meet your sales goals. This does not take into account other variables such as sales cycle length, but it is simple, easy to manage and straightforward for the sales team to understand. I highly recommend asking your salespeople to calculate the load input needed to reach their own sales goals.

Here's an example:

A salesperson has an annual sales goal of $2 million, with an established base business of $1 million. He has an average hit rate of 35 percent.

Sales Goal = Base Business + (New Load Input * Hit Rate)

Sales goal:	$2,000,000
Base business:	$1,000,000
Hit rate on new opportunities: 35%	

Load = (Goal - Base)/Hit rate   Load = (2,000,000 - 1,000,000)/35%

New input load = $2,857,143

Working through the formula, the salesperson needs to identify almost $3 million in new opportunities during the year to meet his sales goal. If we break that down further, the salesperson needs to identify, on average, $238,095.25 in new opportunities every month.

I frequently ask company leaders and salespeople if they know their load input. And more importantly, are they managing it?

This is where CRM can give you instant visibility on how you are doing and provide that leading indicator.

Here is an example of what this might look like in a CRM system.

Figure 6-1: Load Input

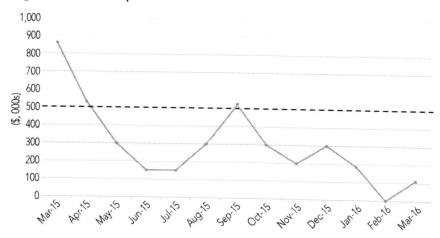

The dashed line represents the load input goal per month. In this case, it's around $500,000. The solid trend line represents new opportunities identified by the sales team, or new input.

Looking at this trend, the company is below the dashed line (the load input goal) for nine out of 12 months. This is a pretty good leading indicator that the bookings in the coming months are not going to be at the level needed to reach the sales goal.

This is also a good example of how pipeline numbers can be misleading. They do not provide an indication of trend and when those opportunities were put into the pipeline. In this example, the three months the company was above the dashed line (load input goal) were 10 months ago. So

Your Leading Indicators

the pipeline might be $10 million, but if you are not trending your actual load input against your monthly load input goal, you won't see the real picture.

When I went through this process with an industrial sales rep and service company, we set up load input goals for all of the key areas that management wanted to focus on, including sales by total company, salesperson and key manufacturer. We got the salespeople involved, which required a change in how they were going to focus and manage their business on the front end of the sales cycle. We reviewed the concept and formula with the salespeople and had them establish their own load input goals based on their sales goals. We set this up in their CRM system and gave them dashboards to monitor how they were doing each month.

We did the following:

- Set the expectations
- Trained on the expectations (how and why)
- Monitored the expectations

We reviewed and monitored the process every month. You could see new opportunities trending up across the board.

Why? Because things that get measured typically are things that get done.

The team seemed to be buying into the concept. We had monthly meetings with the managers and sales team for about six months and decided to stop them in November and December for the holidays. When we picked back up in January, the president said: "Brian, we had our best booking month in 37 years in December." We could have predicted this by looking at the load input against the load input goal trend over the past four months of the year. The company's monthly input trend (solid line) was a good 20 percent above the load input goal line (dashed).

This was their leading indicator, and CRM gave them visibility because they followed the process.

This is a story I tell often as it shows the results that can happen when you focus on things that have an impact on your business. This simple formula results in significant positive impact:

Sales Goal = Base Business + (New Load Input x Hit Rate)

I challenge you to try this within your company. Start by taking the sales goals that you have already established and have your team run those goal numbers through the sales formula. I think your salespeople will be shocked at what their load input numbers have to be.

If you don't have a CRM or know how to set this up, that is OK. Below is a simple Excel sheet you can use to track the input (new opportunities) against the load input goal. After a couple months, you will see what is really going on. This will set the stage for when you do move into a CRM system.

Figure 6-2: Tracking Load Input Goals

Opps	Load Input Goals		Jun	Jul	Aug	Sep	Oct	Nov	Dec
		Month #							
		Month Total $							

The bottom line: Establish this load input goal for the areas of your business that you want to manage proactively: company, territory, products and salesperson. Track the actual new input (opportunities and quotes) against load input goal.

Trend this on a monthly basis, and you will see clearly whether you are heading in the right direction. Is your team finding enough new opportunities to reach the sales goals? If your input trend is going up but still below the load input goal, you may also want to reevaluate your sales goal. Be realistic with sales goals and get your sales team involved when establishing them. I believe in stretch goals, but if goals are too much of a stretch, your sales team will not buy in.

If you have established realistic sales goals, your load input goals are probably in line. If the input trend is consistently above your load input goal, you probably will be heading to the bank to deposit that commission check.

Take control of your sales process. Let CRM be the window into this and put focus on this simple, yet typically overlooked, philosophy. This approach will give your team a competitive edge and give you ROI from CRM.

Sales KPIs

Everyone is trying to get their arms around the KPIs in their businesses. Sales-focused KPIs, which can also be leading indicators for your business, are those that I find most companies leave out.

Think of sales-focused KPIs as the leading indicators that can give you a window into future sales. If you want to effectively manage your salespeople and help them grow their business, identify the KPIs that will allow you to quickly and easily know how they are doing.

The key word here is sales. Most companies are focused on back-end KPIs. Back-end KPIs mean the company is looking at numbers that describe the order and invoicing side of the business. Here are some examples of back-end KPIs:

- Average days payable

- Inventory turns

- Bookings this month

- Invoicing this month

When the controller at your company says your average days payable is around 60 days, you know instantly whether that is good or bad. When you hear that your bookings in the past month were $1.5 million, you know whether this is good or bad. These are typically the types of KPIs being used inside companies today. They have become ingrained in your company and are known and easily graded as good or bad by everyone on the team.

So what are some sales-focused KPIs that you could make part of the company culture that are forward-looking?

- Number of sales visits

- Number of new leads

- Number of new opportunities (discussed in first part of this chapter)

- Number of new quotes

- Open quote dollars (pipeline)

Figure 6-3: Load Input Goal Calculator *Download spreadsheet at ROIfromCRM.com*

Yearly Goal		$2,000,000		Input outlined cells	
Yearly Base Business		$1,000,000		Gray cells are calculated	
Quote Hit Rate %		35%			
Load Input Goal (annual)		$2,857,143			
Load Input Goal (monthly)		$238,095			
		$20,000		Average quote value	
		12		Number of quotes per month	
Sales Visits > Opportunities > Quotes					
New quotes needed each month		12		Sales KPI	
Opps needed for every quote	2				
New opps needed each month		24		Sales KPI	
Sales visits needed for every opp	2				
# of Sales Visits needed a month		48		Sales KPI	

Start with the end in mind. Use the load input formula to calculate the load input goal you need to hit to reach your sales goal. With the earlier example, we established our load input goal was $2,857,143. With this number, we can set some sales KPIs to track.

Note: This spreadsheet can be downloaded at www.ROIfromCRM.com.

Now calculate the number of sales visits, opportunities and quotes it is going to take to reach the sales goal. In this case, we believe it takes two sales visits to uncover an opportunity and two opportunities to get one new quote. This is where CRM comes into play. You can easily track sales visits, opportunities and quotes in CRM. And you can automate this to quickly and easily get these actual numbers.

In this example, the monthly load input goal is calculated to be $238,095. If the average quote is $20,000, you need a rate of about 12 quotes a month. The sales KPI is 12 quotes a month.

If it takes two opportunities to find one quote, then you need to identify 24 new opportunities a month. So another sales KPI is 24 opportunities a month. If it takes two sales visits to find one opportunity, then in this case you need to be making 48 sales visits a month.

Keep in mind this was just an example. Do this exercise with real numbers and see what you get. Sales visits today can also be defined as touch points with prospects. It is not always easy to make direct face-to-face sales calls, but meaningful email exchanges, phone conversations, webinars and so on can count as touch points, as well. In this example, if the sales KPI for sales visits is 48, did you have 48 quality touch points with prospects this month? If CRM is set up properly it can track and report on this very easily.

A possible goal within your company is to establish these sales KPIs so that they become as ubiquitous as back-end KPIs, such as days payable.

When your vice president of sales says your input this past month was 12 quotes, 24 opportunities and 48 sales visits (quality touch points), you will know these are good numbers.

Every salesperson's numbers for new quotes, opportunities and sales visits will be different. The main takeaway here is that sales is a numbers game. You just need to figure out what your numbers are and need to be, including your load input goals.

Again this is where CRM can automate the process. Create dashboards that give real-time feedback on how each salesperson and the full team are doing. And if you don't have a CRM yet, a simple Excel scorecard can get you moving in the right direction.

Takeaways

- Let CRM be your window into your business's future with a fresh approach to tracking new opportunities and setting sales goals using the Secret Sales Formula: Sales Goal = Base Business + (New Load Input X Hit Rate).

- Traditional approaches to a sales pipeline can be misleading. One of the challenges is the quality of data and outdated opportunities.

- Make forward-looking sales KPIs such as new leads or new sales visits as ubiquitous in your business as back-end KPIs.

- A CRM system can automate the tracking of KPIs, providing real-time feedback on whether your business is moving in the right direction.

- Things that get measured, get done. Track your team's progress in areas where you want to see improvement.

Better Data, Better Forecasts

"I don't know how anybody can run their business without a CRM, actively utilizing the strengths of it," says Shelly White, co-owner and vice president of sales and marketing at manufacturer Quest-Tec Solutions. "It would be mind-boggling. How do you put together an account list for the sales guys? How do you track anything?"

White's experience goes back a couple of decades when she first implemented an industry-specific CRM system at her industrial distribution company. The distributor used the CRM to develop forecasts based on input from the sales team and others. "We were fanatic about it," White says. The team wanted to be as precise as possible with the data. The rule: Don't add a quote unless you're at least 75 percent sure you'll get the business.

How could White ensure that quotes and opportunities added to the system were qualified? One tactic was to rank potential business based on a buyer's history. If a potential client had been quoted 10 times but never purchased, the company may as well not have quoted at all. Or sometimes, the company would back out before the quote stage. White also emphasized the importance of purging old quotes after about 18 months to improve the accuracy of the forecasts.

Before automating with CRM, she used what she called a "nondynamic forecast" – basically, submitting data on paper. But there was no easy way to look at past data to compare it with actual results. With CRM, she could easily go back and forth in the system to get the big picture. She could ask why a potential deal didn't close or why a series of quotes with the same customer may have fallen through.

When White moved to her current company, Quest-Tec, a manufacturer of level indicators, gauges and valve product lines, there was no doubt CRM would follow her there. "What it does for a lot of companies is give you a path for success," she says. "… You have to have a vehicle to maintain all of your customer information. Whether it's competitors on a particular project, or the activities you do with these customers, everything is in one central database to keep the big machine going."

Chapter 7

Where to Focus
for Maximum ROI

Remember, the first 30-90 days are critical to your company's success with CRM. Based on the pain points you identified in your CRM Road-map Matrix, consider what to implement or focus on in each stage of CRM adoption. We find that many companies need to start with the basics and build from there. Don't rush it. The last thing you want to do is overwhelm your team.

As a reminder, onboarding typically follows a schedule similar to this:

- Implementation: First 30 Days

- Phase 1: 30-60 Days

- Phase 2: 60-90 Days

- Phase 3: 90-180 Days

Here are some potential areas of focus in your business for each of the above phases, starting with CRM implementation. As we walk through each of these phases, keep in mind that the tasks we include are just examples. You may decide that some of what we discuss in Phase 1 here is actually better suited to Phase 2 for your business and vice versa. Use your road map to design your phases based on what your company needs.

And remember: Start slow and grow. Don't try to do everything at once. Phase 1 as I describe it may seem basic, but focus and excel in these areas and you will start to reap rewards from your investment almost immediately.

Implementation Phase

Where you want your company to go will drive how you set the system up. Make sure the CRM vendor is driving the hierarchy and layout of the system to position it for Phases 2, 3 and 4, not just Phase 1. You don't want to do major surgery on the system when you are ready to move forward with new initiatives.

Think of building a house. In Phase 1 you can't afford a garage, but you know you will want one in the future. Lay the foundation or pilings for the foundation from the get-go so that you can pour the slab six months down the road when you can afford to do it.

In the implementation phase, lay the foundation for all future use of the system.

First, clean your data before you begin implementation. Tap someone to lead the charge on this – a data cop who can serve the data up ready to go for the vendor. Set standards and determine which fields you want to bring over into the new system. Most CRM vendors have templates and can guide you through. Some will help with basic clean-up, such as duplicate-checking. But at the end of the day, there's no way for a CRM vendor to know which data is good and which is bad; that's up to you. Only import what you know is accurate.

After cleaning the data you already have, determine the data you need to capture in your system going forward, which comes back to what you want the output to be. I frequently ask my clients to show me some of the reports they currently use to manage their businesses. That tells me where their heads are at and what's most important to them. That way we ensure that when we set up the system, we're capturing that data. For example, if 30-, 60- and 90-day forecasting is important, that needs to be incorporated into the forecasting module of the system. If you run regular reports by territory, build in automatic territory reporting from the start. Or if you want to track and give reports to your key manufacturers, set that up in the implementation stage, as well.

We want to hardwire and configure the system to automate those pro-

Where to Focus for Maximum ROI

cesses for you so you're not reinventing the wheel every month or every quarter when you've got to run reports. In addition to automating what's already being done, a CRM vendor or consultant should challenge you on ideas you're not thinking about – different ways to use a CRM system that can add value to your business. They need to be able to quickly see where the gaps are.

The better the foundation, the easier your transition will be.

Phase 1

For our example, we will focus on four areas in Phase 1: company management, contact management, activity management and opportunity management. If you start with just those four areas and put processes around them, you can derive a lot of value from CRM.

(Refer to our Lagniappe chapter at the end of the book for tips on setting up the data hierarchy in your system.)

Company management

Your system should include entries for different locations for each specific company. What you're doing for ABC Company in Houston is probably different than what you're doing for ABC Company in California or New Jersey. You need to be able to track and monitor what is going on at each location.

Of course, you should also be able to roll that up into a snapshot of everything that is going on with ABC Company. Some of the key components at the company level that you should track: the business's field of play, the industries they are in, their territories and more. Capture information from their websites. Track social media feeds on that company. What is their annual purchase amount from you? How much are they spending?

Contact management

Manage and track the contacts linked to that particular company's location and those contacts' key information. What's their role? Beyond their titles, what do they do? What is their influence? How do they buy?

Are they economic buyers? Members of the purchasing team? Users? Or high-level decision-makers? This is key because as you start tracking opportunities, you need to ensure you're reaching the proper decision-makers for that opportunity. We won't cover that in detail in this book, but the data you collect on contacts – beyond names and phone numbers – is invaluable.

Activity management

Activity management is tracking every touch point made with a contact and company. A touch point may be a simple phone call or an in-person sales visit. It could be a letter or an email. It may be a service call. (Remember, think beyond the outside sales team!) You have more touch points than you probably realize with each of your customers. Your system needs to be able to track those touch points and capture them by date, as well as who in your company made that touch point. Who in inside sales spoke with John Smith at ABC Company last week? Who made a service call on the company? What did he fix and why? When did the outside salesperson last visit John? This information becomes critical to share and leverage across your team. This is where you will capture ROI from CRM.

But don't just record that a sales visit was made; record the purpose. Was it an expediting call? Was it a complaint call? Was this an inquiry for a special application? Or was it a request-for-quote call?

Also include the product or service the customer called about. During the onboarding process, set up manufacturer product or service codes so that you can slice and dice the data by product category. Many CRM vendors don't talk about this. There's no hierarchy for products in many systems; instead they include it in a "notes" field. Setting up product, service and manufacturer codes gives you much deeper visibility on what's happening in individual lines or what potential issues may exist at the product level.

At minimum, make sure your CRM system has product codes for your high-level categories. When you make a sales or service call and log that activity to John Smith at ABC Company, you should be able to quickly and easily log that the visit was related to products and services that your company wants to track and gain visibility on.

The results of tracking this data can show very quickly which products your team is comfortable with and, most importantly, what they are not comfortable with. It may be a training issue. Or maybe they don't like a manufacturer's line so they don't introduce it. Or the product causes that salesperson problems, so he avoids it.

Right now for many, however, this information is out of sight and out of mind. This is such a simple thing that can be solved with CRM. And your system must first be wired to track and report on this. That goes back to your implementation stage.

Opportunity management

Opportunity management is the entire front end of the sales process. As we discussed in Chapters 5 and 6, opportunity management adds visibility on what's coming down the pipeline. This is your leading indicator. A lot of companies are not doing this, or if they are, they're asking their sales teams to fill out call reports or forecasting reports in an Excel spreadsheet. Automate that process in Phase 1 of your onboarding.

Here are the specific areas you should start tracking:

- Company and contacts involved
- Product or service code
- Estimated quantity for the product or service
- Estimated dollars
- Expected close date
- Next action date
- Next strategic action item
- Stage of the opportunity
- Competition
- Journal to keep information in one spot as you move opportunity

through the process

If your team starts to track touch points, logging the whys of activities and linking them to companies and contacts, as well as product or service codes, you will get the visibility you are looking for. When you plug in opportunities from your outside sales team by product or service with expected close date, competition, opportunity value and so on, that will drive pipeline and forecasting. In most cases, we can automate and eliminate all those Excel spreadsheets and call reports that have been flying around. Bringing all of these pieces together also facilitates a team-selling atmosphere, one in which all departments are suddenly sharing and leveraging valuable data.

In most cases, you can ask your team to do this in one system and not add any more work than they are doing right now in different databases and systems.

Phase 2

What you include in Phase 2 depends on your CRM Phased Roadmap, but here are a few common examples.

Four-Dimensional Account Profiling

In Phase 1, you added the basic but critical information you need to know about a company. Four-dimensional account profiling drills deeper. Most companies do one-dimensional account profiling, calling an account A, B, C or D based on the current business they're getting from a particular customer.

For four-dimensional account profiling, we ask four questions:

- **What is the account's current sales volume with your business (A, B, C or D)?** Assign a dollar value. Each company will typically have a different dollar range for each category. For example, an A might be greater than $100,000 a year in sales, a B might be between $75,000 and $99,999, and so on.

- **What is the customer's potential volume?** Use the same scale as you used for the first question. Is the customer a high-growth account that could potentially move from a C to an A? It's easy to answer the first question based on sales and bookings, but potential volume requires a salesperson to really dive into an account and get his arms around it.

- **What are the current products and services that the customer uses?** Use the product and service codes that were set up in the implementation phase. If you haven't linked those in the system to that customer yet, do so now.

- **What are the potential products and services the customer could purchase from you?** Again, this requires the salesperson have a strong understanding of the account. If the account is in a certain industry or uses certain applications, it may be easy to pinpoint other potential products based on what your other customers use. Link potential products to that customer.

Figure 7-1: Four-Dimensional Account Profiling

			Input outlined cells			Gray cells are calculated	
Sales Scale			**Matrix Ranking**				
A	>$250,000		AA	Stay close 7 days	DA	Highest growth but no products leverage	
B	$150,000	$249,000	BB	Maintain 30 days	CA	High growth with something to leverage	
C	$50,000	$149,000	DD	Last resort	DB	Good growth but no leverage	
D	<$50,000						
Account	**Current Sales**	**Potential Sales**	**Matrix**	**Current Products**		**Potential Products**	
A Company	C	A	CA	Valves, Fitting		Pumps, Motors, Drives	
B Company	C	B	CB				
C Company	B	B	BB				
D Company	B	A	BA				
E Company	C	B	CB				
F Company	D	D	DD				
G Company	C	B	CB				

When you finish answering these four questions, which may require some work on the part of your sales team, build an account matrix to identify opportunities for growth. An account matrix will help you to lump the CAs, BBs, CCs and so on that you identified in the four-dimensional account profiling. It then allows you to put in place action plans and track progress on each of these accounts.

Exercises like this should be simple and straightforward. This increases the likelihood your team will complete them and will give you a far deeper understanding of your customer base. Keep your sales team from spending time on accounts that are cats and dogs (Cs and Ds).

Proactive Opportunity Management

In many cases, companies are practicing reactive opportunity management. The sales teams are simply documenting opportunities as they stumble across them or discover them in the field. This is incredibly important, especially if you're not doing that right now, but in Phase 2, start practicing proactive opportunity management.

First, profile your accounts using four-dimensional account profiling.

After you profile your accounts, identify accounts that are CAs. This means that currently they are Cs, but potentially they are As: high-growth accounts and great targets. An account in this category is already buying from you – the easiest place to get business is where you're already getting business – so start simple. Take a product that this account could be buying from you, but isn't. Log that proactive account opportunity and track it. Build a business plan around how to get that product into that account. (Make sure there's enough potential volume to justify you putting an action plan together.) Designate opportunities like this as proactive versus the standard reactive. Proactive opportunities typically have much longer sales cycles, so it could take a year to ultimately get this product into a facility or location.

Most customers do not know how much you actually offer. They know you by a handful – if that – of products or services. Put into place a plan that changes that.

Of course, there is training that goes along with this and all the other phases outlined in this chapter. I'll talk about that more in Chapter 8. There is also a cultural change required. The person driving proactive opportunity management should be a vice president of sales or sales manager.

Calendar management

Some companies put calendar management into Phase 1. It's a simple thing, but many companies manage calendars in individual Outlook accounts. In a CRM system, you can do group calendaring – and not just internally. You can also track the calendars of external partners, such as manufacturers, product specialists, and so on.

Think about how nice it would be for an inside salesperson to have the calendar of an outside service person so that she knows that he will be at ABC Company next week. The ability to tell a customer on the phone that someone from your company will be stopping by for service (or another reason) and would be happy to come see him is powerful.

Quote management

You may have a quote module built into your CRM system (ideal) or you may continue to quote outside of the system. Reps or distributors often quote in Word or Excel, with a lot of cutting and pasting. Or they might quote out of the ERP/accounting system because they can stage it to be converted to an actual sales order. Some companies use a quote configurator from a manufacturer. However you approach it, quote management is typically low-hanging fruit for improvement in your business.

The challenge with any of these is tracking the quotes. A CRM system lets you track quotes and drive forecasts. At the minimum you can track that this quote was linked to John Smith at ABC Company for this product and assign an expected close date. You can then link the quote document to a salesperson, company, contact, product or manufacturer. The information is put into a shared system, which allows you to leverage this knowledge across your entire team.

Service call tracking

Even if you have just one service person who does work in-house or in the field, he can be an incredible source of insight on the client. But most company service departments are islands with no real link to the sales team or other departments.

If you have a service team, find a way to connect service and sales using the CRM system. Track down to the product line and the specific type of service call. Was it routine maintenance or an emergency call? Then train the service team to ask leading questions and uncover information a salesperson typically can't because the client isn't as open with the sales team as it might be with the service team.

Linking marketing with sales

How do you bridge the gap between marketing and sales? Just as with service and sales, the marketing department is frequently viewed as an island and not really connected to the sales team. This is a huge mistake. A CRM system can facilitate communication and collaboration between the two teams. In Phase 2, you may want to build this bridge.

Make sure that the sales team knows which email campaigns are going out, for example, and to whom so it isn't blindsided when it walks into a client's office. Share how clients are responding to marketing messaging with the sales team. With today's technology, you can track engagement at the customer level online.

Phase 3

What you include in Phase 3, again, depends on your CRM Phased Roadmap. Here are some examples of more complex functionality your team may be ready to implement based on its progress from implementation to Phase 2.

Project management

In industrial and construction markets, projects are large-scale jobs your company may be pursuing that involve a broad range of products and services. The ability to track those in a tool that allows project management saves time and improves efficiency. If projects are a big part of your business, you may consider moving this into Phase 2.

A project may include a new plant expansion or a total revamp of a facility. Projects typically have long sales cycles, and multiple people inside and outside your company are involved. Because CRM allows you to share and leverage knowledge between your teams, it is an ideal tool for project management.

Manufacturer visits

A pain point for many distributors and reps is managing visits by manufacturers. Consider developing a process with CRM to communicate and collaborate on those manufacturer visits. Back in the day, my company represented 40-plus lines. At any given time, we would have three to five manufacturers making sales calls with our team. Managing that could be a nightmare. Using your CRM system and a calendar that shows just vendor visits, everyone can be on the same page. This also shifts the responsibility for the productivity and effectiveness of those visits to managers instead of the sales team.

If you know about all opportunities associated with a manufacturer's products – thanks to the data you've collected in your CRM, you have a window into where you should spend your time when that manufacturer visits. Use expected close dates to prioritize those appointments. What's more, if your inside sales team has started to track all expediting or service calls for that manufacturer's product, you also have a road map of where you can do damage control.

Thanks to your CRM system, you have the information you need to make good business decisions. Now it's not chaos. It's organized, and you've got a plan.

Demo tracking

Another lagniappe area (a little something extra) is using your CRM to track demos and other resources. At BGI, we could have built a small chemical plant with all the demo equipment in the trunks of salespeople's cars. Set up a demo category in CRM to track equipment (model number, serial number, salesman, company the demo was left with).

Using the CRM to track this gives the other salespeople visibility so they can easily exchange demo equipment.

ERP integration

ERP integration is the Holy Grail. When you do this, you have a complete system. You have front-end management via CRM, and you have back-end data via the ERP, from orders to credit holds to inventory levels. When a salesperson visits ABC Company, he can see that front-end, as well as actual orders, including orders that are on hold. While the value is clearly there, many companies don't step up to the plate to make it happen. It is a big commitment in both time and money.

It may seem counterintuitive to wait until Phase 3 to integrate your CRM system with your ERP. Some companies want to do this in Phase 1. But because of the complexity of the integration – the massive amounts of data, the additional training that it requires, the number of people involved – it's better to start simple and train on the CRM system itself and to build up to the 360-view that the integrated system would provide. Your team is already anxious about CRM; don't prolong that with a more complicated kickoff.

Remember, every company is different. Go back to your CRM Phased Roadmap to drive what you include in each of your phases, and set the timeline for each phase for what will work best for your company.

Use this plan to communicate with your team on what to expect going forward.

Keep the philosophy of start slow and grow through all of the phases. Pick a couple of things – maybe three at most – to add as you move from Phase 1 to Phase 2 and from Phase 2 to Phase 3. Give your team time to acclimate to each part of the system. You're throwing a lot at the users, and you're trying to change the culture at the same time. Do it right, and you'll find that the process will be much less painful than you expect. Implement ongoing training and tweak the CRM solution as needed.

Recently, I worked with a company on a conversion to a new CRM

Where to Focus for Maximum ROI

system. Rather than make the entire system available to each of the team members, we hid everything from their dashboards and brought out only the tools we wanted them to focus on at any given time. I didn't want them to turn on all of the capabilities and have the team be overwhelmed with tools they weren't trained on.

That said, take care you don't start slow and *never* grow. Build on your successes, win buy-in and maximize your use of better sales processes and technology.

Takeaways

- Plan for the future use of your CRM system early on so you don't have to reinvent the wheel six months down the road.

- Wait to link your CRM system with your ERP to simplify the transition for your team, but make sure that you put the wiring in place at the start to facilitate the eventual integration.

- Clean data is the foundation upon which all other CRM functions are built. Be sure to prioritize data before implementation. In fact, it's best to start with fresh data than to import bad data.

Recommitting:
A Phased Approach

New Gen Products, a valve distributor, automation center and manufacturer's rep firm, started business in 2010 and grew rapidly. But it soon fell into the same trap many companies do after building a solid base of business: It concentrated on the low-hanging fruit and took its eye off the future, according to CEO John Mulvey.

In 2013, New Gen Products realized it needed a better approach and invested in a cloud-based industry-specific CRM solution. It used just a small portion of the capabilities from the start. But the distributor knew that if it wanted to truly get ROI from CRM, it would need to commit more fully.

"While we implemented a CRM a few years ago, we were not utilizing it to its full capacity, and we realized we needed to change in order to keep up," says Debbie Gray, vice president. "In the last year, our management team recognized we needed to become proactive in lieu of reactive."

New Gen Products moved to the next level in 2015. "The first thing we had to do was to get our management team on board to understand the CRM capabilities in detail and the time commitment it would require from our sales staff," Mulvey says. "Once we truly understood the opportunities, we decided to make the time investment."

New Gen Products approached CRM with fresh eyes. It started by dividing the implementation into three phases:

Phase 1: Getting all the data it needed into the CRM program. "Garbage in is garbage out, so the accuracy of the data was imperative," Mulvey says.

Phase 2: With the data correct, the company focused on developing management reports that would give the leaders the ability to see call activity and the sharing of data between inside and outside sales teams. Reports also provided insight for the sales team.

Phase 3: The company has yet to move to Phase 3, but the goal is to hone its forecasting capabilities, run reports on vendors and look at which products its sales force is most focused on selling.

Mulvey says a recommitment to CRM requires hard work. "If your sales force is not committed, and you can't convince them on the long-term benefits the CRM can bring, it's probably not worth the effort." But New Gen Products has been able to move forward with the team on-board, thanks to a focus on sharing CRM's benefits. "After six months of dedication to the program, our management team is convinced this has been worth the effort, and we see it increasing sales and gross profit now and in the years to come."

Gray agrees. "We are continuing to expand our reporting abilities, and with that we are able to have a clear vision for the future."

Chapter 8

Training on the Why,
Not Just the How

Not surprisingly, one of the top reasons CRM does not gain traction for industrial distributors, reps and manufacturers is culture. The chances of success when your team is not on board are low. When you are changing the way you approach sales, you should expect some pushback. This is hard and can be painful, and many employees will not be ready. As the leader and evangelist of CRM within your company, always look at it through the eyes of each user. Always ask the question users are asking: "What is in it for me?" They need to understand how a new sales process and supporting CRM technology can help them do their jobs better and ultimately sell more.

Companies need to invest in training – not just at the start of implementation, but throughout the first year and beyond. A critical part of the onboarding we discussed in Chapters 2 and 7 is training. You are setting your business up for the success of your CRM, so don't skimp.

It's not just training on *how* to use the new system; it's training on *why*.

That's the missing component for a lot of CRM companies that train users. They train them on how to add a new company and contact, create an activity log or create and manage an opportunity. Or they focus on which form or tab to use to do this or that. But frequently the missing component is why the company implemented CRM. What's the value it will provide your team?

For example, clicking a button allows a service person to see this follow-up call. Or it allows a salesperson to get a report that shows all opportunities by customer and expected close date, helping you to prioritize each day. Or when you click on this product code in your activity log, it helps the managers better plan manufacturer visits and answer questions from manufacturers when they call.

In nearly every training session I have conducted, the first question I ask is: "Why do you think your company is moving forward with CRM?" Typical answers are:

- So they can monitor what I am doing.

- They want more information.

- They need reports.

When asked "What is your company's competitive edge?" without fail, they give the same answers:

- People

- Products

- Service

- Experience

The problem is that those are the same answers everyone, including the competition, gives. Which means none of those things really provides a competitive edge.

The why of training your team on CRM is to give a real competitive edge. The CRM system can help your team:

- Better manage the front end of the sales cycle.

- Put in place systems and processes to share and leverage information within the team.

- Separate your business in the eyes of manufacturers on how you manage your business. As a rep/distributor you are nothing more than a 30-day contract. I used to tell our team all the time that we needed to make sure our manufacturers viewed us as their best sales channel.

The more you can explain to your team why they are doing this, and what a particular process enables, the better off your company will be. You want every member of your team to see the bigger picture. That's how you get ROI from CRM.

When you focus on the why and not just the how, you will have more buy-in. Show them the value of shifting to a focus on the front end of the sales cycle will do for the company. Have your team do some exercises showing that there are gaps in the communication between all departments and what filling those gaps with CRM can do for the company. Help them understand how a single click can add incredible value to the team.

Who?

Don't turn the training over to the IT department. That doesn't mean don't involve the IT department, but IT shouldn't drive the training. IT should not be the primary champion because typically the training will shift to a how rather than a why mindset. What's more, the IT department may not understand the why from the perspective of sales and service for the simple reason of never having been in a salesperson's or other employees' shoes.

But someone has to own the training responsibility, and it's important to identify who the best person is for that role for your company. There are multiple options out there, including resellers, CRM vendors and CRM consultants. A CRM vendor will typically take the how instead of the why approach unless you've taken a more consultative approach with them; then you're more inclined to get the why. That said, at the end of the day, it is up to the company to promote and drive the why. I suggest a company have at minimum two internal champions who can also be responsible for ensuring a consistent message before, during and after implementation.

Admin champion: This person or team is responsible for getting the CRM system ready for prime time. This person will typically be in IT and will work with the system setup and oversee the critical task of data cleanup and import. This person will make sure all users have the correct system permissions and access information. The admin champion likely will focus more on the how than the why.

User champion: This is the most important person for a successful CRM implementation and its subsequent success. Ideally, this person holds a sales management position and can drive expectations while keeping the why in the forefront. This champion also typically has a big stick to enforce expectations. As the title of this book indicates: This is about sales process, not just technology. This champion needs to drive sales processes and focus for the CRM.

The user champion, as relates to training, should:

- **Set expectations:** This is typically done at the beginning and during the implementation phase. But as you get feedback from the team and move from phase to phase, you will also need to reinforce these expectations.

- **Train on the expectations:** This needs to be ongoing. As I noted in Chapter 7, integrate user training across all phases of onboarding, and incorporate follow-up after onboarding in the form of Q&A and other formats.

- **Monitor expectations:** Let your team know that you are monitoring the input and management of the system. A good friend of mine, Reed Stith, used to say to his team: "If it isn't in the CRM, it didn't happen." This was his way of letting the team know that he was monitoring the usage. You wouldn't dare go to one of his sales meetings and say something about a customer issue or big opportunity if it were not already in the system. This reinforcement is important to the success and growth of the company.

Timing and Roles

During implementation, the user champion and the team members selected to pilot or be involved from the beginning should be trained. Ask your CRM provider to let these users get into the system on the front end as it is being built. The members of this team can often serve as trainers themselves. Make sure they are respected by their peers, that they understand the system and that they're drinking the Kool-Aid. They need to preach the virtues of the new system. This is all part of training.

After your pilot team is trained, the system set up, and all data, forms and workflows tested and approved, it is now showtime. I recommend onsite training for the initial training if possible. Start with the why. Have the user champion or someone with sales management in their title give this presentation. This will set the stage going forward. After the why, share the phased approached that will be used for implementation (as outlined in Chapter 7) and then focus on expectations for Phase 1. This makes the process clear for everyone, with no surprises.

That critical 30- to 90-day window when you first implement CRM will dictate whether CRM will be as successful as you want it to be.

Ongoing Training

After those first 60-90 days, don't stop. Training is not a one-time event. After the initial training, backfill with Q&A training sessions once a week or once every other week. Take a half-hour to an hour for your team to ask questions after they've had a chance to use the system.

You need to provide this feedback mechanism. This makes your team feel like they're part of the process, rather than poorly trained and thrown to the wolves. Your team can provide valuable feedback, which can be used modify the system. Face it, you might not have thought about everything at the start.

Have one or two CRM champions who your team can go to within the company on an ongoing basis. Typically the sales manager will drive the expectations and have a couple of champions to reinforce and make sure everyone is trained and following the processes that were set up from the start.

And never stop reinforcing the why, which can get lost in the day-to-day after the initial burst of activity around the new system.

Takeaways

- To get your team on-board, train on the why, not just the how.

- Training doesn't stop after you hit the "go" button. Continue to reinforce the why and the how of CRM long after implementation.

- Encourage feedback on what's working and what isn't with your CRM system. This will ensure the system works for your business, not against it.

Sales Training as a Byproduct

If you have laid out the sales processes and built your CRM with these improved processes, your team members will be trained every day they use the system. Implementing these processes reinforces the why.

An example of this is opportunity management. As I mentioned in Chapter 5, build questions into the CRM system that the salesperson should answer to qualify and move an opportunity forward using the Ws:

- Who are the decision-makers?

- Who else is being considered as a potential vendor?

- What is the reason the customer wants to purchase this product or service?

- When will you need a formal proposal?

- What is the decision process?

- What is your next strategic action and when?

When you meet with your salesperson or in meetings, monitor their answers and progress. By doing so, you will reinforce the expectations of the system and improve how that salesperson goes to market.

Chapter 9
Considerations in Vendor Selection

If you don't already have a CRM system but are ready to move forward, you need to select a vendor. Or maybe you aren't happy with your existing CRM system, and you're ready to throw in the towel and find a new one. If so, you're in the right place.

Selecting a vendor might be the hardest and most confusing part of the equation. This chapter will not tell you which CRM provider you should select. That would be unrealistic. What this chapter will do is get you thinking about what to look for and how to evaluate CRM vendors. My goal is to arm you with information and best practices to help you make the best decision for your company.

Where do you start? The easy answer is "Google." But do you know how many CRM options show up when you Google "CRM software"? CRM has become a commodity due in part to the rise of cloud-based offerings, which have helped spark widespread adoption. While businesses used to be nervous about adopting a cloud-based software solution, it's now commonplace, especially for niche systems such as CRM. The price keeps coming down and the number of features keeps going up. That sounds like a good thing for the consumer, doesn't it? Not necessarily. When I give talks and ask the audience who feels they are actually getting ROI from CRM, the average number of hands raised is less than 20 percent of those with CRM. Why? Because companies feel they can just buy any CRM, implement it and it will work for them. But it doesn't work that way. It's about process, not just technology. Don't overwhelm your team with features you don't need or that don't fit your industry.

The key is building a solution around your business, not building your business around the vendor's offering. It's always easier to have the system bend around your practices than the other way around. Base your specifications document and your vendor evaluation on the homework you've already completed in this book. Your goal should be to fill the gaps you've uncovered in the Sales Process Review and CRM Roadmap Matrix. When developing your needs list for vendor evaluation, use a phased approach. Share where you want to start and where you want to end.

When you engage with vendors, provide them with your company's back story and the challenges you want to solve. There's no question the vendor will give you plenty of information on the features and benefits it offers. But by telling the company your story – how you interact with the systems you have today, your work force makeup (remote, mobile workers, personas), the needs of various departments – you're pushing them to think of their systems in the context of your needs.

Share what you uncovered in your Sales Process Review and outlined in your CRM Roadmap Matrix. Ask the vendor whether it thinks it is a good fit. Some will revert to sales mode and instantly tell you yes. But ask them to use the information you provided in your examples to get a more customized sales pitch on what you're looking for.

Let's review what you should consider when evaluating potential vendors:

Demos

The first demo will cover the basics: the features and benefits the software provides. The second demo should address your specific needs and provide an opportunity to revisit features from the first demo or ask questions to clear up any concerns you might have about this vendor. Make sure everyone on the CRM evaluation team participates in all of the demos and fills out a scorecard. If anyone is missing from any of the demos, you can create dissension and won't have an apples-to-apples comparison between systems.

Here is a sample of an evaluation scorecard. This does not include your features wish list, but it does address some basic and important things to include in your evaluation.

Figure 9-1: CRM Evaluation Scorecard *Download spreadsheet at ROIfromCRM.com*

Key Factors (rank 1 to 5) Vendor:	1	2	3	4
Company				
1. Years in business				
2. Success in our industry				
3. Local support				
4. Hours for support				
Technology				
1. Open Source				
2. Open API				
3. Built in integration modules to standard ERPs				
4. Outlook integration				
5. Google apps integration				
6. Export to Excel				
7. Integration with 3rd party email marketing				
Software				
1. Ease of use				
2. Expandability (can it grow as our company grows)				
3. Online help				
4. Integrated reporting and charting				
5. Mobile app				
Onboarding				
1. Programs to help us identify where we should focus				
2. Onboarding process and procedures				
3. Program for after initial training to keep moving forward				
4. Training program				
5. Online training documents and videos				
Other				
1. Do I feel our company can work with CRM provider				
2. Do I feel CRM provider can bring value				
3. Do I feel CRM provider truly understands our business				
4. Does CRM provider have user council				
5. Is CRM provider investing in technology				
6. CRM provider process for prioritizing new development				

After each demo, have a follow-up meeting with your evaluation team as soon as possible. Take an immediate vote to get a feel for where your team is at – a simple thumbs-up and thumbs-down vote is sufficient. If everyone says thumbs down, it's an easy dismissal. If it's all thumbs up, that vendor will likely move onto the next round. Using scorecards provides an objective way to keep moving forward. It's really easy to get analysis paralysis with such a big decision. Establish guidelines that can help you get to your final two vendors so that you can do true due diligence for an informed decision.

CRM partner vs. provider

You should not only be looking at selecting CRM software, but a CRM partner. This is critical if you want to get true ROI. Unfortunately, this is where many companies fall short. They spend most of their vendor evaluation time on features. But it's just as, if not more, important to ensure the CRM company you select will be a good partner. Will the company bring value to the equation or is it just selling you software?

Bigger is not always better. Think more broadly, and select up to five vendors to evaluate. Develop a simple scorecard to keep track of performance throughout the process. Remember, this is not a one-time relationship with your CRM vendor. You should be planning for a long-term relationship with a good partner.

How do you know if the CRM vendor courting you is the right fit? First, ask a lot of questions that require more than just a simple yes or no answer. Challenge the CRM vendor. Don't just look at today, look down the road. Ask the vendor to give you an idea of where it's going. How does it prioritize its features and future development? How does that align with your CRM road map and where your company is heading? Does the vendor bring ideas and real-world stories and examples to the table?

During the courting process evaluate the vendor's follow-up. Does the vendor say what it is going to do and when it will do it? Does it actually follow through? If it can't get this right during the sales-pursuit stage, what will its follow-up be like after securing your business?

At the end of the day, do you feel comfortable with the vendor? Do you feel like you can work with it for the next couple years? If you don't feel comfortable during the evaluation stage when the vendor is on its best behavior, it is probably not going to get better after the honeymoon is over.

Value added resellers vs. direct sales

Confirm how the CRM vendors you're considering go to market with sales and support. If it's through third-party channels, there may be additional considerations.

When buying direct from the software provider, that provider will have better access to development teams for customization and a better and broader picture of its solution and the issues you might run into. Buying direct also may result in better pricing for you, as you may be able to ask for pricing breaks or incentives, which they have more control over.

A value added reseller, or VAR, is essentially a distributor of software and the customer's touch point with the software brand. A VAR implements the software and trains users. A VAR can be just as much of a partner as the software brand itself can be. The value of a VAR to a small client is that the VAR may be able to better get the attention of the actual software company than you could on your own, if needed. A VAR may also specialize in your industry, taking a more generic software package and customizing it for other clients like yourself. The goal is to find the right partner for your business. Most VARs are not getting rich on the sale of software; instead, they make their money on customization and training.

There are pros and cons to both the direct and VAR approaches. Understand the differences and what those mean to your company. Of course, you can't control how the CRM vendor goes to market, but understanding it can help as you go through your evaluation process.

The cloud vs. on-premise

Many of the solutions you'll find today for CRM are cloud-based, providing your team with the ability to access the data and solution anywhere it goes. One factor you must consider is Internet connectivity, which is a primary driver of performance, especially for salespeople on the road who might not always have reliable connections. The good news is this is becoming less of an issue. Many systems offer offline access via mobile apps, and it's becoming difficult to find a spot in this world where you can't get Internet between 4G and Wi-Fi availability.

With cloud, you'll usually get an up-to-date solution. There are no big upgrade processes as with an on-premise solution hosted on your own servers and computers. In other words, you won't need to buy the same software over and over again every three to four years. If there's an update, it's typically included. Cloud-based solutions also tend to be more reliable and have more functionality and security. In all but the largest and most technical firms, a cloud-based solution will offer greater security and reliability than an on-premise solution because most vendors have greater resources than your internal IT department.

That said, not all cloud providers are created equal. A lot of it is the function of experience and expertise and how much history an organization has. More established companies may have advantages over new entrants, but not always. Consider this as you evaluate your potential vendors.

References

The vendors you evaluate will be more than happy to provide you with good references. If not, that is a big red flag. But vendors are likely to provide you with only positive reviews. Ask those references for additional references. Word of mouth or references from others in the industry are worth their weight in gold. Also look at a vendor's support website, if it has one; you can usually find candid comments from actual users in discussion forums on what's working and what's not. If the vendor has an app, look at app store reviews. That's an easy way to get feedback from actual users and not just the person who led the purchasing process or a manager. You can also use online industry analysis, such as that provided by Gartner, but remember that some vendors pay to be part of some of these programs.

At the end of the day, take references with a grain of salt. Use them to confirm – not make – your decision.

CRM vendors

Your goal may be a comprehensive solution or, based on what you uncovered in the exercises in this book, a simpler solution to tackle specific needs. Find the right balance for your organization. You will want the ability to flex the software around your business, but you want the minimal amount of flexing possible.

The ideal situation is to get as close to an out-of-the-box solution as possible to meet your needs. It will be easier to use the software from the get-go, and you will have a greater chance of success. That's why an industry-specific solution rather than a broader solution may be a better option for many companies.

Benjie Pieper, president of distributor Trivaco, recently selected an industry-specific solution for this reason. "We have been looking into CRMs for the past several years but have been hesitant on pulling the trigger for multiple reasons, including the cost. But it was primarily because our industry is unique and we just did not get the feeling the software companies we were dealing with totally understood what we were looking for."

Don't just think about your needs today, as we discussed in Chapter 7; look at where you would like to be 12 to 24 months down the road. Make sure your CRM vendor will be able to get you there. Selecting a vendor is probably the hardest decision you will make. This is not a one-time date; you're getting married. Good luck and choose wisely.

Takeaways

- Selecting a CRM vendor is one of the most important decisions you make. Think of a potential CRM vendor as a partner, and not just as a software provider.

- Have your CRM Roadmap Matrix ready to share with potential vendors so that they know what you're looking for from their software.

- References should be used to reinforce your decision, not make it.

- Make sure your evaluation team represents all departments, and that each member attends each demo of each potential vendor to ensure an apples-to-apples comparison.

- Use the Evaluation Scorecard to consistently score potential vendors.

- Bigger vendors aren't always better. Find the solution – large or small – that's right for your business.

Chapter 10
Next Steps

So you've gone through the SalesProcess360 CRM Audit and you're sold on the importance of a better sales process and the value CRM can bring to your business. What do you do next? Use this chapter as a checklist for your company's next steps.

This book was designed to provide insight on adding value with CRM whether you currently have a CRM system or not. This chapter is divided into two sections: no CRM and with CRM. Skip to the section that applies to where you are in your CRM journey.

No CRM
Review the list of reasons CRM fails or succeeds in Chapter 4. List the challenges that your company in particular may face. Your Top 5 will likely be different from the company's down the street. And be honest with yourself. For example, is the average age of your workforce 50, making adoption of new technology a challenge? Maybe your sales team doesn't have laptops? Culture is likely to be included on your list. Every company struggles with the culture change required to make the shifts outlined in this book. Accept that it is tough and will take time. Culture is the No. 1 reason that CRM fails to succeed.

Assemble your CRM evaluation team. Make sure the team is cross-functional. Don't just pick people who you know will be successful with CRM. Find evaluation team members who are nay-sayers and will challenge the status quo. Don't forget to include the top guns, the top salespeople who are respected by their colleagues. Include representatives across departments, including inside sales, marketing, service, etc. Your team must reflect the real world for it to be effective.

Complete the SalesProcess360 CRM Audit outlined in Chapter 2. There's a reason this step comes after you form your evaluation team;

your team should play a key role in completing this for an accurate view of your business and the gaps you need to fill with CRM. Remember, this audit will find the red flags – the gaps – and the low-hanging fruit you can tackle right away.

Create specifications based on the CRM Roadmap Matrix and Phased Roadmap. Many companies write out what amounts to a wish list. They present several pages of features and benefits, but they don't provide guidance on what is most important. The problem: You've essentially skipped a step and gone from forming a team to writing a list without considering the questions answered by the Sales Process Review. In your specifications document, list your needs in phases based on what you prioritized in your CRM Phased Roadmap.

Your specifications should be based on needs across the company, not just one department. Develop your list with your cross-functional team to avoid a list that leans in favor of any one department. In addition to not overwhelming your team, taking a phased approach with your specifications list gives your potential CRM vendors a much clearer view of your company's priorities and goals with CRM, as well as what you will need on the technology front to accomplish those goals.

Put together a list of CRM companies to consider. Look for vendors with success in your industry. Ask other companies in your industry at trade shows and conferences. Hundreds of CRM providers would be happy to pitch your business; it can be overwhelming. But a bigger provider is not always better, so resist the urge to go with the major brand names if it's not the right fit for your business. Put between three and five providers on your list. If you add more, you risk analysis paralysis – or difficulty in making a decision because there are too many options. Read Chapter 9 again for considerations in selecting a vendor.

Create a simple evaluation scorecard that can be used by your CRM evaluation team during the demos. See Chapter 9 for a sample scorecard.

Set up demos with the CRM vendors. Make sure everyone on the CRM evaluation team participates in every demo to ensure an apples-to-apples comparison. This also ensures that when a decision is made, no one can say they never saw the demo.

After each demo, conduct a follow-up meeting with your evaluation team. Get everyone's feedback and rank that vendor. Your goal is to get your list down to the final two for due diligence.

Have a more detailed demo with your final two potential vendors. Review your evaluation scorecards and have the vendor address any areas of concern. The odds of a vendor getting all green checks on your evaluation scorecard is slim to none. During this stage really dive into the onboarding/implementation, training, support and future product development. Ask about user groups, and how the vendor prioritizes future development and features. Really try to get into the vendor's head and figure out what makes the company successful – and what will keep it successful so that you can grow with the company. Visit references if you can. Ask the reference for other companies that are using the system. This is not a one-time deal. You are getting married to this vendor. Be sure you are making the right choice.

You have negotiated a good deal and made your decision. Now the real game begins. Reread Chapter 7 and develop a phased approach to implementing your new system.

Assemble a pilot group. This should again be a cross-functional group. Here are the key things to focus on:

- Have a phased approach, and don't try to do too much too soon. Don't go to the next phase until you've checked off the existing phase, despite your original schedule. In other words, be sure that you are seeing success with your current efforts before moving forward. (Chapter 7)

- Start with the end in mind and build the foundation for the future. For example, if you know you want to integrate with your ERP down the line, be sure the plumbing is in place from the get-go. You will know where you want to go because you've already outlined your phased approach.

- Don't skimp on training. Train on the why not just the how. People won't get it the first time around. It's important to reinforce your message. (Chapter 8)

Have monthly or quarterly progress meetings to get feedback from your team. Management must be in these meetings. Move fast on any modifications that the team decides should be made. If the team knows that feedback results in changes – that it won't go into a black hole – buy-in will be that much stronger. Expect that changes will need to be made when the CRM is being used in the real world. Nothing is set in stone after you hit the go button.

Remember where you started. This process is tough. You will find yourself asking: Why am I doing this again? Stay focused on the big picture and where you are going. But occasionally look back and remind yourself of how much you've accomplished. Sometimes we forget about the progress we've made.

Lead by example. Show the value. Your team will appreciate your involvement and in the end it will reinforce the company's commitment to this growth initiative.

With CRM

Be open to change with your CRM. If you are reading this book, you recognize you have room for improvement, so it's time to get back on track. If you're not ready to throw the towel in on your current CRM system, keep reading. But if you are ready to start fresh with a new system, go back to the start of this chapter and read about the steps to take as if you were starting from scratch with no CRM.

Assemble a cross-functional team to drive the CRM refocus project. Don't just make your team up with outside and inside sales. Look at service, marketing, customer service, operations and so on. Take this opportunity to expand the use of CRM in your company. If you are like most companies, you probably didn't follow the detailed process outlined in this book when you first implemented CRM so there is likely a lot of opportunity for improvement.

Review your current focus, processes and use of CRM. Conduct the SalesProcess360 CRM Audit (Chapter 2) and look for gaps and areas for improvement. Get your team involved. They have been using the system and can tell you exactly what is or isn't working.

Document the feedback and come up with a list of gaps or areas of improvement. Use the CRM Roadmap Matrix and Phased Roadmap (Chapter 2) to determine which areas you will refocus on first.

Meet with your team and determine the two to three areas you will refocus on. Design a new phased approach (Chapter 7). Look for some easy wins – some low-hanging fruit.

Recommit to training. Because your team has already been using CRM, training on the why is more important than ever (Chapter 8). You will still need to train on how but the why will pull this all together for your team. In most cases, a lack of training on the why is why the CRM was probably not as successful as you had hoped. And if you are taking a new approach altogether to CRM, training will be critical to success. Your team may need to be resold on CRM.

Have monthly or quarterly progress meetings to get feedback from your team. Management must be in these meetings. Move fast on any modifications that the team decides should be done. If the team knows that feedback results in changes – that it won't go into a black hole – buy-in will be that much stronger.

Lead by example. Show the value. Your team will appreciate your renewed focus and in the end it will reinforce the company's commitment to this growth initiative.

Chapter 11
Conclusion: It's Your Turn

You want to reach the next level of your business. How do you get there? How are you making sure your team focuses on the right things? I regularly ask this of the distributors and manufacturers I work with.

The answer is in this book. Think about it: If you did some basic blocking and tackling on just a few of the concepts we discussed, and used CRM to its potential, what could that mean for your business?

My goal for this book was to keep it simple and to the point. I shared best practices learned over the past 18 years of working with companies on CRM selection and implementation.

But as passionate as I am about the value CRM can bring to your business, let me be very clear:

Do not move forward with CRM in your company if you are not ready to change the way you have been doing business and the demands you have set for your team.

The *process* I've outlined in this book is not easy. In every company I have worked with, changing the culture from top down has always been the highest hurdle to success.

You know the statement: You have to put in to get out. CRM is a prime example of this. You will have to put in a lot of work on multiple fronts – the greatest among them culture – but the payoff will be there if you're willing to do so. As a leader of your company, I challenge you to commit. Drive the CRM project. Don't sign the contract and then go stealth.

Here are the key takeaways I hope you got from this book:

CRM is about processes – not just technology. If you could focus on improving just two things in your company with CRM, it's these:

- Focus on the front end of the sales cycle. Put processes, procedures and visibility on the part of the sales cycle that can drive growth. Use the SalesProcess360 CRM Audit to identify the areas you need to focus on the most.

- Put in place processes to share and leverage knowledge across your team. This is where CRM can shine.

Start slow and grow. Don't try to do too much in the beginning with your CRM. Pick three to four areas to focus on first. The SalesProcess360 CRM Audit is a great way to figure this out.

Sales needs to be the driving force behind CRM. Don't turn this over to IT to drive and manage.

Get a cross-functional team involved early as you evaluate and ultimately roll this out.

Position CRM as a company-wide team solution that can bring value to everyone, and not just the sales team.

Look at a potential CRM vendor as a business partner, and not just a technology vendor. You will be married for a long time.

CRM can be a leading indicator for your business if implemented properly.

A successful CRM implementation must start with improving your processes. I will go to my grave believing that we took the family business (Breard-Gardner Inc.) from less than $10 million to more than $30 million in fewer than seven years because we used CRM to improve our sales processes and created a team-selling environment.

You can get **ROI** from **CRM.** It's not an oxymoron. I believed it so much that I left a very successful family business to pursue my passion to help other companies do just that.

I want to personally thank you for purchasing this book and truly hope it brings value to your company whether you are just starting to evaluate CRM solutions or you already have CRM and need to refocus.

I will leave you with one of my favorite quotes:

> "The only way to do great work is to love what you do. If you haven't found it yet, keep looking. Don't settle. As with all matters of the heart, you'll know when you find it."
>
> *– Steve Jobs*

I truly love what I do, and I'm glad I got to share my experience on what has and hasn't worked with you. If you believe you can get ROI from CRM, I believe this book can give your company a competitive edge and help you take your business to the next level.

Acknowledgments

My goal for this book was to make it an easy read with real-world examples and exercises you can immediately apply in your company. I have distilled my 30 years of sales experience, including 18 years of developing a CRM system for industrial sales organizations, and the best practices I've learned along the way into these chapters. I've worked with more than a hundred companies on improving their sales processes and use of technology.

People ask me all the time: "Do you miss being in industrial sales?" My answer: "I never left. I am just involved and coming at it from a different angle."

This book is dedicated to my father, Doug Gardner, and his partner, Charlie Breard, who gave me the opportunity at Breard-Gardner Inc. to get into the business of industrial sales and sales management. To my dad, I know it was not in your plans for me to leave the family business, but I can't thank you enough for your support and the opportunity for me to pursue my dreams. I would not have accomplished nearly as much or gotten to where I am today without you. To Mr. Charlie Breard, CVB as he is known, thank you for your support and teaching me the value of note-taking and the art of follow-up. You were the master.

I would also like to thank my partners in crime at BGI, Danny Wedge and Michael Johnson, for putting up with me, the SOB (Son of the Boss). They were great and always treated me as one of their own. They supported my ideas and the changes I wanted to incorporate at BGI. As a team we had some exciting times, growing the company from less than $10 million to more than $33 million – all internal growth. A lot of those changes are included in this book. Without the support of my father, Charlie, Danny and Michael, this book would not have been written.

I would also like to thank Mario Igrec, my partner with whom I started Selltis. Mario helped me see how technology and sales process could come together to add value to companies. I have never met a person more detail-focused and smarter then Mario. He kept me on track and was able to take my passion for sales process and apply it to technology.

Thank you to the distribution, rep and manufacturing executives who shared or inspired stories, examples and best practices in this book, including Jeff Baker, Dave Lefley, Benjie Pieper, Chad Hammerly, Joe Incontri, Shelly White, Steve Molinari, Keith Rainwater, John Mulvey, Debbie Gray, Reed Stith, Mario Porrata-Franceschini and Chip Toth.

And I can't thank my wife Alexis enough for believing in me over the past 25 years. Leaving the family business was a very tough decision, but she supported my passion and belief in what I was doing.

Thanks for purchasing this book, and I hope it brings value to you and your team.

Brian Gardner

Lagniappe
Setting Up Your System

Growing up in New Orleans and Southern Louisiana, we had a culture of always offering a little "lagniappe" – a little something extra. Sometimes I would go to get a dozen doughnuts and come home with 13. In other parts of the country they call that a baker's dozen; in Southern Louisiana we call that "lagniappe."

I hope the content in this book challenged you about the ROI you are getting from CRM if you are already using CRM, or it gave you a road map for doing so if you are thinking about implementing CRM.

Consider this chapter your 13th doughnut – some additional tips and tricks on how to set up your CRM system.

The way you set up the data in your system can have a big impact on the ROI you get from CRM. For companies that sell multiple products or services, I recommend the following three-level hierarchy in the CRM for reporting and visibility. For a rep/distributor, this is real world. A manufacturer might want to substitute product family or a higher classification level for the manufacturer branch.

Manufacturer/product category

- These three levels (manufacturer, product code, model number) need to be separate categories and linked in the system as a parent/child hierarchy. This will give you the ability to report by model and product and roll-up automatically to the manufacturer.

- If you are not quoting out of CRM, you might not need this down to the model number level.

- Link the product code category to all other categories in your system. For example: When you are logging an opportunity in your CRM, you will want to easily link the product to the opportunity.

Figure L-1: Manufacturer/Product Tree

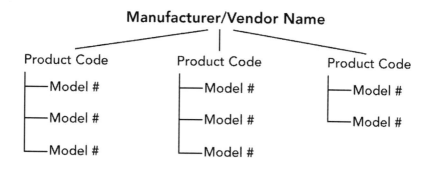

Company category

For each of the companies in your CRM system:

- Track industry activity. You will want to be able to slice and dice all of your activity (touch points, opportunities, successes, applications, etc.) by industry. Keep it simple. Track just the industries your company targets. Most companies don't need every NAICS codes.

- Track target accounts. Include a simple "target account" check box so you can filter and report on just your target accounts.

- Profile accounts. At a minimum, profile your accounts using the standard A, B, C or D. Using 4-dimensional account profiling will let you go even deeper. Read more about this in Chapter 7.

- Parent/child hierarchy. Group and link all parent/child company locations. For example, link Shell corporate (parent) with all the Shell locations (children). You will need the ability to see down to each location but easily roll up all the activity for the parent.

Contact category

- Categorize contacts by their buying roles. For example, economic, technical, user, financial, etc.

- Have the ability to prioritize contacts. For example, use A, B, C or D or 1, 2, 3 or 4.

- Build and see contact hierarchy, including who reports to whom.

- Classify key contacts and track their how frequently they are called on. John Smith may be a 14-day, while Bill Jones is 30-day.

Activity management

Have the ability on an activity log to link the product codes that were discussed during that activity.

Track all the activity, or touch points, by your team with contacts and companies, including:

- Phone calls placed and received
- Sales calls
- Service calls
- Emails (most CRM systems can link with Outlook and Gmail)

Track the purpose for the activities, which may include:

- General inquiry
- Expediting
- Complaints
- Returns
- Success

How powerful would it be to easily get a report on all the complaint phone calls your inside sales team has taken the last 30 days for a certain product? If the manufacturer is coming to visit, you can show it all the complaints your company has been fielding for its products.

Leads-Opportunities-Quotes

One approach to tracking leads, opportunities and quotes is to make all of them part of the opportunity category in your CRM system. The idea is to create different stages for your opportunity within your CRM: leads, qualified opportunities and quotes. This simplifies things and drives all pipeline reporting from one category.

Lead category

Structure a lead by more than just a contact. Include:

- Which product or service the contact is interested in.

- The source of the lead (trade show, web, seminar, etc.).

- Priority ranking.

- Next action and date.

- A central journal area for keeping your notes in one location.

Opportunity category

You may link each opportunity to a single product/service for visibility and reporting at that level. An opportunity should:

- Be linked/associated with both a company and contact.

- Be able to link to more than one company or contact. You may need to track multiple companies and contacts involved in an opportunity, especially with projects, including an end user, engineering firm, contractor and so on.

- Be linked/associated by a product/service, allowing you to slice and dice your opportunity pipeline by product/service.

- Link more than one user or team member.

- Have a Go% and Get%. A Go% is the probability the opportunity will go forward and move to an order. A Get% is the probability that you will get the order.

- Have an expected close date. This drives accurate forecasting

- Have a next action date. This can be used to automatically prompt the salesperson to take action.

- Have a next action. Have your salesperson document what his next strategic action is.

- Include a competition field to list who you are up against for the business.

- Include a central journal area for updating the opportunity with new information.

- Include a reason that opportunity was won or lost.

Quote category

A quote should:

- Have the ability to link to multiple companies and contacts.

- Track who put together the quote.

- Track the inside and outside salespeople assigned to the quote.

- Include an expected close date.

- Include a next action and next action date.

- Include a central journal area for updating with new information.

- Include a reason the quote was won or lost.

- Have the ability to clone or duplicate a quote.

Figure L-2: Project-Opportunity-Quote Tree

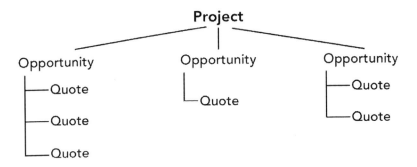

Projects

In the pursuit of sales, a project is typically a longer, more complex sale that includes multiple opportunities and multiple parties. Your project should:

- Link more than one company and contact.

- Link more than one user (team member).

- Link more than one opportunity to the project.

- Include a next action and next action date.

- Include a central journal area so that everyone involved with pursuing this project can update their information.

Resource or equipment tracking

Many companies also use CRM to track activity with resources or equipment. This may include:

- Demo equipment

- Preventative maintenance scheduling

- Service technicians

Expense Tracking

Most companies just have the salesman fill out an expense Excel sheet with where they spent the money, expense total and maybe a notes area. Tracking expenses in a CRM can automate those expense excel sheets and give you more reporting capability. With a CRM you could look at linking:

- The company(s) for the expense

- The contact(s) for the expense

- The manufacturer and/or product that was discussed

- The opportunity, project or quoted that the expense was related too.

Just think of the reports and visibility you could have on where your expense dollars are going. Are they being spent on the companies, contacts, manufacturers, products and sales opportunities they should be spent on?

Example: We spent $3,000 last year promoting a product line that only brought in $10,000 in sales at a 20 percent gross profit margin. We are $1,000 in the red and didn't even know it.

Example: We spent $5,000 last year on expenses at the Dow Baton Rouge location and our annual sales for that location were only $20,000 at a 22 percent gross profit rate. Do the math.

For more resources on CRM and sales process, check out my website, salesprocess360.com.

About the Author

Before co-founding Selltis in 1999, Brian Gardner spent more than 20 years in technical and industrial sales in the process control and instrumentation industry. As the vice president of sales and marketing, he led efforts to double sales at a distribution/representative firm on the Gulf Coast in just a couple of years through an internal focus on sales process. Gardner founded SalesProcess360 to share best practices and help companies think differently about sales process and CRM.

Praise for Brian Gardner

"A CRM is a considerable investment and in order to realize the return we wanted we felt the need to change our process on the front end of the sales cycle. This is where Brian's expertise and experience comes into play." – Benjie Pieper, Trivaco

"With this book and his system, Brian Gardner brings his unique talent for making the complex simple. He has the experience, with family business, in the world of industrial sales professionals and a full set of practical steps that will benefit all involved in their quest for winning in sales!" – Mario Porrata-Franceschini, MRF Inc.

"Brian is a dynamic presenter who really knows what he is talking about. If you are a distributor, representative or manufacturer in the industrial equipment sector, you will benefit greatly from Brian's insights on sales management and customer information systems optimization." – Joe Incontri, Krohne Inc.

"Brian has always been a passionate yet practical evangelist for sales process and focusing on the front end of the sales cycle. What he teaches and coaches is so relevant to any industrial manufacturer, distributor or rep firm. What I really love about Brian is he knows that the behavior and discipline of the sales team is what is important – technology such as CRM merely enhances good fundamentals. He also knows how to get salespeople to adopt new methods – because he's been there himself." – Reed Stith, industrial growth expert and former manufacturing executive

"I've been hoping that Brian would put his vast experience as sales process guru in a book form ever since he and I cofounded Selltis. That dream has come true and the world is richer for it. First through Selltis, then through SalesProcess360, sales professionals have benefited from Brian's wisdom for almost two decades. Now they have a volume that speaks of his passion and belief in applying technology and sound sales practices to improving their sales processes. Thank you, Brian!" – Mario Igrec, co-founder, Selltis

"I first met Brian Gardner while I was working for his father at Breard-Gardner Inc. Brian, Michael Johnson and I were all promoted to vice-president positions. In our new roles, we all contributed to sales management, and Brian took a particular interest in understanding the sales process and how it could be improved. We all knew that tracking opportunities early generated better results, but Brian wanted to develop a process by which we could measure these results. What started as a handwritten form documenting sales opportunities soon migrated into a spreadsheet, and from there, what eventually became Selltis. At first we were just tracking opportunities, but Brian wanted to track the entire sales process and has now made a successful career of teaching others how to do the same." – Danny Wedge, John H. Carter Company

About the Author

About Gale Media, Inc.

Gale Media is a market-leading information services and publishing company. Its two business units – Modern Distribution Management and MDM Analytics (formerly Industrial Market Information) – provide knowledge products and services to professionals in industrial product and wholesale distribution markets.

Since 1967, MDM has been the definitive resource for distribution management best practices, competitive intelligence and market trends through its twice-monthly newsletter, market intelligence reports, books and conferences.

MDM Analytics provides proprietary market research and analytic services to profile market share and account potential for industrial products.

For more information, visit www.mdm.com.

Made in the USA
Middletown, DE
18 January 2018